HEN

AND THE ART OF

CHICKEN

MAINTENANCE

Reflections on Keeping Chickens

Martin Gurdon

THE LYONS PRESS
GUILFORD, CONNECTICUT
AN IMPRINT OF THE GLOBE PEQUOT PRESS

Copyright ©2004 by Martin Gurdon

First Lyons Press paperback edition, 2005

The Lyons Press is an imprint of The Globe Pequot Press.

10 9 8 7 6 5 4 3 2 1

Printed in the United States of America

ISBN 1-59228-770-0

Library of Congress Cataloging-in-Publication Data is available on file.

First published in 2003 by New Holland Publishers (UK) Ltd
London • Cape Town • Sydney • Auckland

www.newhollandpublishers.com

Garfield House, 86–88 Edgware Road, London W2 2EA, UK

80 McKenzie Street, Cape Town 8001, South Africa

14 Aquatic Drive, Frenchs Forest, NSW 2086, Australia

218 Lake Road, Northcote, Auckland, New Zealand

Copyright © 2003 in text: Martin Gurdon
Copyright © 2003 in artwork: New Holland Publishers (UK) Ltd
Copyright © 2003 New Holland Publishers (UK) Ltd

Publishing Manager: Jo Hemmings
Senior Editor: Kate Michell
Assistant Editor: Rose Hudson
Design: Ian Hughes, Mousemat Design Ltd
Production: Lucy Hulme
Illustrator: Greg Poole

ACKNOWLEDGMENTS

To David the Dad and Jane the Wife.
Thanks for the encouragement/observations/help/positive bullying.

This book is dedicated to the memory of George Bishop, who didn't know about chickens, but knew about words.

Con

tents

HEN
AND THE ART OF
CHICKEN
MAINTENANCE

The Hows and Whys

THE BUSINESS END

"Would you mind holding the chicken?" asked the expatriate Australian vet as he snapped on the rubber glove.

I picked up Edith, the bird with the defective bottom, in such a way that her wings were clamped tightly to her sides as the vet inserted a strategic index finger. I'd never heard a chicken go "Ooooooo" before, but I had every sympathy with this one.

Edith was a hybrid bird. A standard issue, broad-beamed egg-laying matron, with a rolling gait, an endless appetite for worms, and a certain dignity, which her current predicament was undermining.

"Hmmmm," said the vet.

Edith gave me a baleful "things-couldn't-get-any-worse" look. Then my mobile phone rang, its glissando, synthetic trill echoing round the bare-walled operating room.

"Would you like to get that?" asked the vet. Had there not been a chicken between us he would have been pointing at me.

I had a strong, tasteless vision of letting go and seeing the sickly Edith pivot and end up with her scaly legs waving in the air, or the vet yowling in agony as the weight of his avian patient broke his finger.

"It's alright. The phone's on ring back," I said. Thankfully, the vet did not pick up on this unintended double entendre.

Afterwards I paid $19 [All conversions to $ are approximate based on a rough conversion rate of £1=$1.50] for what was a

slightly inconclusive consultation and wondered, not for the first time, at the turn of events that had led to my days regularly being filled with events like this.

SOFTENING UP

Having a few hens at the bottom of the garden was supposed to be a bit of fun, a mild distraction, but was fast becoming a life-changing experience. It had started with an apparently innocent remark from my wife, Jane.

"You'd like to keep chickens again, wouldn't you?" she said.

This wasn't the first time she'd uttered these words, and I began to suspect an agenda. Jane has a knack of insinuating things into our lives by stealth. She'll offer a vague-sounding thought on a vacation destination, the replacement of a piece of furniture, or the state of my shoes. It will take four or five repetitions of the "vague" idea for it to percolate into my brain and for me to realize that there's nothing vague about it at all. A softening-up process is taking place.

I hadn't kept chickens since I was 10, and a good quarter of a century had elapsed since. I'd spent my formative years in suburban Kew, south-west London, not a place noted for its livestock, but when my mother became ill I was packed off to live with an aunt and uncle in rural Lancashire. My relatives must have been feeling indulgent, or possibly slightly deranged, when they agreed to let their nephew have some birds on the

condition that they didn't roam the garden and pillage the vegetable plot and flower-beds, and that I wasn't to have a rooster, because of the noise.

As it happened, the chickens escaped all the time, pecked holes in vegetables, murdered plants, and excreted acidly and lustily all over my aunt and uncle's lawn, leaving little brown patches of dead and withered grass. One hen ended up nesting under a rather nice shrub, where she raised a litter of chicks—an indication that the rooster ban was not a success either.

EARLY LEARNING

My original flock had been a motley crew of limping, bare-bottomed, ex-factory farm burn-out cases and the odd bantam, bought with money earned collecting eggs at the local factory farm (this was the 1970s)—where my most knackered birds came from.

Used to existing in very small cages in very warm sheds, these hens found the adjustment to much cooler, relative freedom difficult to take. I had three. Of the two scruffiest, most pathetic-looking senior citizens, one expired on the first night, the other lasted barely a week. The third, a stout, off-white authority figure, who'd unwisely retired from egg-laying, was made of sterner stuff.

The factory farm referred to her as a "cull." I handed over 30 cents, hoisted her from a crate of hens earmarked for a soup

manufacturer and called her Ethel. Decades later I have only vague recollections of most of the birds I owned at the time, but I have quite distinct memories of her.

The same applies to Fred the rooster. He was a multicolored, one-eyed troubador chicken who liked a wild time and was prepared to travel to get it. He was a jungle fowl, which meant he had extravagantly curling tail feathers and plumage that was a mass of golds and greens. Fred was a male bimbo with spurs.

He'd escaped from another farm or chicken breeder and taken up residence at the factory farm, where he'd grown sleek on a plentiful supply of layer's mash and spent his leisure time

7

seeking out and screwing the occasional escapee. Fred had successfully avoided being caught by the farmer's two stocky teenaged sons, who would clomp uselessly after him bellowing, "I'll kill that! I'll wring its bloody neck!" This was a fast fowl.

I kept seeing Fred out of the corner of my eye, as a flash of color in the far reaches of a shed or vanishing round the side of a barn. I began thinking covetous thoughts about rooster ownership, and wheedled away at my aunt and uncle about what an attractive bird he was.

Quite why they relented is a mystery; perhaps there was some negotiation about tucking my shirt into my underpants (my aunt was pro, I was anti), perhaps they thought I'd never catch him.

It took weeks but I managed it, and when I did he proved to be totally bonkers, battering me with his powerful wings, slashing with his spurs, and pecking viciously. It hurt, but I hung on. The farmer, a man of infinite patience, let me put Fred in a wire cage with the aged broilers I'd acquired as his girlfriends. He even kept a straight face when I added some grass cuttings to the cage, to remind the rampant Fred of the great outdoors.

After moving Fred into his residence (a hovel made of old bricks and corrugated iron, surrounded by a wobbly wire fence) he was able to experience the real outdoors. As my chicken-keeping experience improved so did the quality and longevity of Fred's amours, and he became less manic and would even feed out of my hand, but he would not curb his wandering ways.

Fred's early-morning routine involved eating, fornicating furiously, then flying over the fence and scuttling off to the house down the lane, where their free-range chickens were given breakfast later in the morning. Here he would have seconds, wink his liverish eye at various members of their flock, and engage in further copious shagging before hotfooting it back in time for tea with us, some post-prandial sex and then bed.

I thought this was rather enterprising, but there were complaints, especially as summer arrived and, with it, Fred's love-children.

"Can't you do something about that chicken?" asked our exasperated neighbor, who didn't want her flock to get any bigger, and did not view the plague of small Freds and Fredas that were now running about her yard with any pleasure.

I tried doubling the height of the fence, which proved no obstacle to Fred, so I took a large pair of kitchen scissors and clipped his wings. Fred just flapped the resultant stumps harder, kept escaping and carried on as before.

As the flock of love-children increased, the neighbor gave up complaining and eventually developed a grudging admiration for her exotic-looking visitor.

Fred had surprisingly good road sense for a chicken. When I banged the food tin he'd hurtle roadrunner-like along the side of the lane to get his dues. But having one eye didn't help and he was eventually hit by a car.

As I scraped his mortal remains from the road I was sad, but also seized by a certain cold-eyed pragmatism 10-year-olds are capable of when viewing death. This was something that happened to grandparents with their parchment skin and to chickens who didn't look where they were going. It was remote and frightening, but rather interesting, too.

FRED II AND ETHEL

I reasoned that Fred had been struck down doing his own thing, and anyway he'd produced a successor, a youthful, slim-hipped version of himself who lacked the urge to travel. With staggering originality I christened this bird Fred II. One of the

disadvantages of being more sylph-like was a certain frustration in the bonking department when making the intimate acquaintance of big-hipped birds like Ethel. Consummation required the avian equivalent of doing the splits, a look of pained concentration, and then frustration when he fell off—a regular happening. Nature is a wonderful thing, however, and Fred II persevered.

Had Ethel been human, she would have worn tweeds, had blue-rinsed hair and been keen on blood sports. She was a control freak who would stomp around the run letting everyone else know that in life's pecking order they were there to be pecked. Egg-laying appeared to be something she did under sufferance—it got in the way of eating or yanking the feathers out of somebody else's neck.

Ethel became ill after I'd introduced a very pretty black bantam, which the other hens turned on and chased away—and with good reason. This bird was diseased, and by the time it died a number of the others were starting to keel over. When the indomitable Ethel began to look off-color I decided to take her to the vet, which was a five-mile bike ride away. It didn't occur to me to ask my aunt or uncle for a lift. Getting a chicken into the saddle bag of my cousin's elderly bicycle took some maneuvering, but eventually she was strapped down, with head and neck protruding. Hens have fixed expressions, but somehow their faces let you know when they're nonplussed.

I don't suppose the trip did Ethel much good. I didn't have an appointment and I hadn't got any money, but the vet saw me anyway, handed over some yellow pills, and I pedalled home again. Ethel was not a good patient. She spat out the medication and, despite my best efforts, the bug got her in the end. So, when she finally died I dug a hole for her and began to consider a suitable replacement.

INDUSTRIAL CASUALTY

There were exceptions to this passive childish callousness, like the crippled hen whose name I've long since forgotten. She also came from the factory farm and was the sort of bird that by then I'd learned to avoid. She was another sad little Medicare chicken with a skinny frame. There was plenty of loose pink skin on display as she'd given up growing feathers on large parts of her body, and she couldn't walk. In fact, she couldn't stand up. The cages had sloping floors, tapered at the ends to allow the eggs to roll out and be collected. Grotesquely, some birds tried to wriggle through this letterbox-sized gap and would get trapped, cutting off the circulation to their legs. It was usually a death sentence.

This chicken was an obvious basket-case, but I decided to take her on. It was winter when I took her home and I half expected that she wouldn't survive the night, but in the morning she was reclining on her straw bed, blinking and looking surprisingly perky. Her disability meant she had to be fed and watered inside

the run, and I had to fend off the other chickens who were keen to help themselves to her grub. The others also took time out to peck the top of her head. Hens have a Thatcherite enthusiasm for market forces or natural selection. If you're ill you're a liability to the flock. A bird that couldn't walk was an unwelcome addition.

This hen, however, was determined. She remained sprawled on her bed and refused to die. After a couple of weeks I began to wonder if this was a permanent state of affairs. Then I noticed her clenching and unclenching the claws of one of her feet. Three days after that she stood up on one leg and began the process of exercising her other foot. Soon she was hopping and limping around the run, and it wasn't long before she made a full physical recovery and even began laying eggs again. Growing feathers wasn't really her forte and she retained the look of a bingo-playing grandmother with alopecia, but when the time came to give up my flock she was one of the survivors I had to re-house. I suspect she lived well into her dotage.

GROWING PAINS

I said goodbye to my chickens in the mid-1970s, when Harold Wilson was prime minister and Ford was still making the Cortina. The intervening years involved incarceration in a vegetarian co-educational boarding school. I screwed up my education and was virtually expelled, moved to London, did badly at college, and then worked as an optician's bike messenger before getting fired.

I sold garbage bags over the phone for two wonderfully manic women, who sacked and re-employed me three times. After that I delivered photographs in Fleet Street for the Press Association news agency, became a hopeless public-relations copywriter, was laid off, and found a job cleaning the loos in a pub.

After getting fired from a car bookstore, I became a journalist and wrote about personnel officers, dead meat, sewage pipes, and sometimes even crooked local councilors. I lived on a houseboat and started writing about cars.

My grandmother died, I got engaged, my mother died. I got a mortgage. I married. Hens played no part in any of this. I thought about them only when Jane made that insinuating comment that secretly I'd like to keep some more birds.

We were at the top of the garden when she said, "You could turn that old cold frame into a chicken run."

I am allergic to all forms of DIY, especially carpentry, but I live with someone who carries a tape measure in her handbag, along with a notebook and pencil, so that things can be planned. Soon we were measuring and scribbling.

"We'd get five or six hens in there," I said.

"And we could have one of those arks and move it around the garden in the summer," said my wife, whom I soon discovered knew how much they cost and where we could buy one. She also seemed suspiciously well informed about who sold chickens.

"So," she said, "when can you start?"

Preparation

RESEARCH

The sort of chicken-keeping we were embarking on can be summed up as: "twee" and "middle class."

Not for us the pragmatic purchase of birds who would lay lots of eggs and then be sacrificed for the dinner table. We wanted hens as pets. They would have names and would stick with us until they fell off their perches—literally, in some cases.

Jane and I were urbanites who moved to the country, and our indulgent approach to the hens who came to live with us was to prove baffling and, frankly, hilarious to our neighbors.

Before the hens arrived we did some research, visiting a county show and peering at what were described by aficionados as "fancy chickens." We saw bantams with bulbous, wart-like combs and red, heart-attack-victim faces. We saw birds with giant feathery flares or little fountains of feathers growing from the tops of their heads, giving a sort of bouffant effect. Both Rod Stewart and Eurythmics' Dave Stewart wore similar coiffures circa 1985.

There were caged, twittering, pigeon-sized bantams, pooping frequently and diminutively into beds of straw that seemed to remain weirdly clean. Anxious-looking hens milled about like frustrated rail commuters, while their stunted male companions stood almost on their toes when crowing with lustful, high-pitched screeches.

At the other extreme, giant, vaguely dinosaur-like birds blinked at the passing human traffic. We saw one enormous

rooster absently tread on one of his blowsy girlfriends, who looked irritated but apparently couldn't work up enough energy to move.

Feathers shone, wattles had a just-scrubbed freshness. We suspected chicken grooming and speculated how this might be achieved.

The people showing the birds all seemed to be ladies with print dresses and old boys with sideburns. They were kind, quietly enthusiastic, and seemed happy to dispense free advice.

We itched to find a cardboard box and take home a Heavy Sussex, but managed to resist (with many birds costing between $37 and $40 each, frugality played a part here). We did invest, though, in several chicken-keeping books to get an idea of what sort of birds we should eventually buy, and what constituted appropriate housing for them. At one extreme we found sweet but slightly rose-tinted DIY jobs offering advice on how to turn your plot into a birdy nirvana. They all seemed to be illustrated with line drawings of oddly smiling chickens sitting in flowerpots or peeping coyly from beneath posies of flowers, and promised endless egg collection for cute, tiny children. Nevertheless, they also proffered sensible advice, such as making sure that chicken-keeping was legal (in some urban areas it isn't, and house deeds can sometimes forbid it), and basic information on the pros and cons of various breeds.

At the other extreme there were sober-looking paper-backed tomes filled with revolting descriptions of chicken ailments. These books were peppered with grainy black-and-white photos of deformed, defective, or, frankly, dead birds.

However, these books of doom also often featured line drawings of those oddly smiling chicken faces, but this time attached to knotted-looking intestines.

DIY don'ts

Having investigated the literary merits of chapters with titles such as *What can I catch from my birds?* and *Droppings*, and having considered ailments ranging from "blackhead" to "fowl cholera," I shuddered and set about building a chicken run. This involved the construction of a large nest-box covered in roofing felt (a bad move, we discovered later) and featuring a platform on which to lay eggs and a perch. The platform and perch were detachable to allow access to the floor for the purposes of turd removal, a task assisted by a hinged lid. There was also a front door so that the hens could be kept inside and the foxes out. The ensemble was completed by two rat-proof ventilation slots. Chickens are prone to respiratory diseases, so good air circulation and a lack of dampness are essential elements of any hen-house.

The result looked surprisingly professional, and I approached the construction of the chicken-run's enclosure with the practiced complacency of someone who is genetically programmed to be useless at practical things—and who never learns from his mistakes. Then an inner voice told me to prepare to visit Screw-up City.

Even before starting, my psyche had been dunked in a toilet bowl of gloom, its head held under as Fate pulled the chain. This was because I'd been forced to go to a hangar-like DIY store to buy fence posts, those sharp-ended metal whatnots called Metaposts (you bang them into the ground and use them to secure the fence posts), a great bale of chicken wire, and a variety of nails and catches.

These places always put me in a foul mood. Perhaps it's the willfully inane music piped into every echoing recess (come the revolution, liking Chris de Burgh will be declared illegal and carry the death penalty), interspersed with pseudo regional DJ voices drivelling on about the price of hovering mowers, woodstain, or repugnant garden ornaments at never-to-be-repeated sale prices.

I feel vaguely sorry for the staff, who mostly seem miserable, simple, bored, or lobotomized. Then there are the other customers. These places are crawling with identical families. Shuffling persons with pendulous lower lips and sour expressions, hell-bent on purchasing case lots of pink insulation.

The hordes seem to have disgorged from slightly soiled white or metallic gold 4x4 cars with personal number plates for people called "ROZ," "ROD," and the like. Unusual names you'd want to advertise. As these monogram junkies clomp from racks of hard board to tins of paint stripper they are rude to each other and vile to the staff. They probably love one another really

and they have done nothing to me personally, which makes me feel guilty and even more cross about the antipathy I feel.

I returned home with a stress headache and murder in my heart. Neither of these things were conducive to successful chicken-run building. Disaster and personal injury soon followed.

After accidentally bludgeoning some tender extremity with a club hammer, or piercing aging flab with a splinter or a piece of wire, a particular home-made swear-word gets used. Sadly, that word is "fuckshit." Quite often it is preceded with "Aaaaagh!" Cruel friends have been known to mimic the cry. They don't regard it as the agonized bellow of a soul in torment. No, they think it is funny. When I am building something outside, my wife goes indoors and closes the windows. And so it was with the chicken run.

I needed a sledgehammer to knock in the Metaposts but, of course, only had a dwarfish club hammer, which wasn't really up to the job. Much sweating and impotent hammering later (viz. Thud!Bang!Bang!Bang!—"Aaaaaghfuckshit!"—Bang!Bang! Clonk—"youBASTARD!"—Bang!Thud!Bang!, etc) and these were more or less battered into the ground at variously exotic angles. This meant that the fence posts themselves jutted out in different directions.

Badly cut bits of 2-inch x 1-inch timber were inexpertly nailed onto these uprights, creating a sort of box-like frame with perspectives and angles that would have pleased Salvador Dalí.

21

Attaching the springy, resistant chicken wire to this so-called frame involved various bits of wood attempting to part company with each other, further self-laceration and torn items of clothing. I then struggled with willful horseshoe nails designed to hold the chicken wire in place, but which bent or pinged into the vegetable patch, never to be seen again.

Bleeding only slightly, I turned my attention to making a door, which ended up looking very nearly as good as the nest-box, but was, naturally, just a couple of inches too large for the door frame.

There's an old carpenter's saying: "measure three times, cut once." I try to adhere to this, but still manage to screw up. The solution in this instance was to do an expletive-laden war dance round the offending item, stomp into the house, drink a large, filthily strong cup of tea, tear the door to pieces, chop a bit out of the middle, and finally, mercifully, finish.

It wasn't pretty and it wasn't clever (this could apply to both the hen-house and its builder's behavior), but we now had a sort of cold frame/aviary at the bottom of our garden. A kind of deluxe prison with a decent view of the vegetable patch. All we needed now were some inmates.

First Flock

A SHOPPING SPREE

We first saw Elvis from a distance. A fast-moving black form on the horizon. At the time we didn't know that Elvis was going to become Elvis. She was just a pretty, slightly butch chicken scuttling along the edge of a field.

We'd answered a newspaper ad placed by a chicken-breeder who seemed to keep birds because she liked them rather than as a means of making a fast buck (or "cluck" perhaps?). She lived on a farm located down a dirt track about three quarters of a mile from a National Trust-owned castle in Kent, where her husband looked after the grounds. You had to drive through the castle grounds to get to the farm. As we got closer, their home seemed to roll over the horizon and revealed itself to be a sort of gingerbread cottage.

Clasping a cardboard box to carry home our birds, we emerged from the car to be greeted by a red setter with a wet, inquisitive nose. The dog was soon joined by a phalanx of kittens, a goat on the end of a long tether, and the sound of a great many chickens chickening about. There was also an angelic-looking small boy who told us in lugubrious detail about a chicken that had recently expired.

"Have you anything in mind?" asked the breeder.

"Er," we said. "Not really."

She led us past chicken arks containing maternal-looking hens surrounded by swarms of professionally cute chicks and

exotic bantam roosters with small clusters of girlfriends. "For breeding," explained their owner.

Then we came up to the main enclosed area, a huge, muddy expanse with a couple of small ponds, surrounded by staked, orange plastic fencing and a low electric fence. Behind this was a sort of chicken and duck city.

THE AUDITIONS

The choice was bewildering, and we wandered among this squawking, quacking horde failing to make a decision on the basis that if you went for one bird you liked, another even nicer one might be missed.

We both saw the stocky bantam with the pretty gray and brown plumage. She looked extremely steely-eyed and was not keen on being caught, but after much running and flapping around the breeder cornered her and pounced.

We'd wanted a hen that would lay large eggs, and had soon tracked down a standard issue, brown hybrid farm bird with the stance of a sumo wrestler. She proved surprisingly speedy and was highly displeased when she failed to escape. She was stuffed reluctantly into the cardboard box already occupied by the bantam. There was much unhappy scrabbling.

Both of us had seen the putative Elvis when we'd first arrived, and when she was unwise enough to hurtle into view again we said "That one," and the chase was on. I think it must

have taken about 10 minutes of frenetic lunges, lurches, and near misses. Elvis was fast on her feet and had a rugby player's skill of sidestepping you at the last minute. At one point, as she hurtled into a nearby field, we nearly gave up. But being incredibly dumb, even for a chicken, Elvis turned round and ran back again.

When finally run to ground, she turned out to be extremely fetching, with a big red comb, wobbly wattles, and an attractive green tinge to her feathers.

"That isn't a rooster?" we asked. "No, no, definitely a hen," said the breeder as the bird who would be Elvis was plunged into the cardboard box.

Hen number four was another bantam, living with three or four similar birds in one of the breeding arks.

An ark is a Toblerone-shaped portable chicken enclosure, with a bedding/nest area at one end and a wire-mesh run at the other. We'd decided to buy one of these as well, to put on our lawn so we could have the pleasure of seeing the hens near our house and so that they could have a break from the hen-house. It cost about $75 and required a lot of manhandling to get it onto the roof of the elderly Volkswagen station wagon I was driving at the time. I forget how much the hens cost—about $37 to $45 for the four, with the bantams being individually more expensive. The one thing we did not acquire was a rooster. At the time we were living in the middle of a row of terraced cottages, and at least one of our neighbors, who'd spent a lifetime in our village and knew about

these things, had said politely but firmly that she would not view living next door to a bloke-chicken with any kindness.

We sympathized. The idea of a feathered maniac using the small hours to bellow at every other rooster within a half-mile radius that he was both well hard and well hung and "Do you want some then? Because you're going to get it," was one that we decided would be good to avoid.

PECK OR BE PECKED

Having got our avian booty home and manhandled the ark onto our lawn, sorted out a bowl of water and some food, we released

the foursome into their new world of gentle, genteel spinsterhood. They went straight for the food, beaks making "Ting! Ting! Ting!" noises on the metal bowl. They clucked and cried softly and contentedly. It was a scene of friendly domestic bliss. We said "Aaaah," or something equally nauseating, and sat on a garden bench to watch this happy scene.

The brown chicken bent down and began tentatively pecking at the lawn, a sweet image that was soured somewhat when the beady, gray-brown bantam viciously pecked the back of her head. In fact she took a beak full of feathers and wrenched them out. The brown hen screamed in a very satisfactory way. Encouraged by this success, the bantam set about the other two birds. Soon there was an orgy of hysterical running about, feather-pulling and anguished cries.

In between being brutalized, the other hens carried on eating and scratching. They also took to having a go at each other. The brown hen pecked the black hen and the other bantam. The black hen also went for the other bantam, but left the brown hen and the sadistic bantam alone. The other bantam didn't take a pop at anybody and spent most of her time dashing about inside the run looking sore and harassed.

This was nature's way of saying "Screw your bucolic fantasies, a pecking order's going to be established here." It took a mere 10 minutes to sort out the divide between the peckees and the peckers.

CHAPTER

Hens at Home

JUDGING BY APPEARANCES

"How can you tell one hen from another? Aren't they all exactly the same?" asked a friend.

Given the raw material that goes to make up a chicken this is a fair question. From a distance, a flock of hens has all the individuality of a parade of army cadets. Having tiny, primitive brains and operating as a flock, chickens tend to react to each other and their environment in much the same way. It's a survival mechanism as much as anything else, but to the uninitiated that does make them all seem identical.

Live beak by jowl with them and this perception soon changes. The first bird we owned for whom a name suggested itself was the bantam with the megalomaniac tendencies. We called her Bossy Chicken. Given her fascist-dictator style of hen management, we could equally well have called her Il Duce (or Mussolini's Missus, maybe?), although she was rather more skilled at getting her own way than the bald Italian dictator.

When I let the chickens out in the morning, Bossy would ensure that everyone was given a good pecking before they were allowed to eat. Food was something she always got to first. This viciousness was mutual as it extended down the pecking order, with the other bantam being the recipient of everyone else's opprobrium. Eventually, this poor persecuted hen learned to

hang back while the others pecked their grain and each other. Then she'd totter forth and eat.

During the day, the sounds of generally contented hen activities would be punctuated by a scream of pain as Bossy dispensed instant justice for some terrible crime, viz "You are standing on a piece of mud where I want to stand," or "Don't you know who I am?" People who work in customer service centers, telemarketing operations, and the editorial offices of some tabloid newspapers will be familiar with similar management techniques. The fact that Bossy was a third smaller than two of her victims, who could easily have knocked her off, didn't seem to occur to them or her. She exuded a natural authority. At the start, I was silly enough to try and intervene.

"Don't do that!" I squeaked. Occasionally I would even clamber into the run and have a half-hearted go at roughing her up, jabbing at her with an index finger. I had the daft idea that she might come to see me as higher up the pecking order than her and so leave the other birds alone. No such luck. Bossy regarded these interventions with uncomprehending, cold indifference, and carried on as before.

Edith was a name that almost demanded to be applied to the stolid brown chicken. She had an Edith stance, and a handbag-swinging demeanor for which no other name would do. Had

she been able to wear glasses they would have been tortoiseshell-framed and horn-rimmed.

We called the black hen Elvis as a very oblique reference to k. d. lang, singer of whom Madonna once said, "Elvis is alive, and she's beautiful."

Elvis the chicken was beautiful, too, but sufficiently butch for some people to ask if she was a rooster. The fact that she

started to lay eggs on an infrequent basis tended to imply that she wasn't, but Elvis soon confused the issue by semi-crowing, particularly if she was irritated, excited, or stressed. Elvis was highly strung, and this was something she was keen to vocalize. Actually, she could half crow, managing a strangulated "Cock-a" but failing to get out the "doodle-dooo!" bit at the end. Occasionally she'd get pretty close. Stretching herself like a length of pre-tensioned knicker elastic, she'd screech, "Cock-oooo-a-oooowa-aaaagh!" Then Bossy would peck her.

On winter mornings I'd clomp to the top of the garden to let the chickens out of their nest-box (we'd shut them in at night as extra protection against predators) and would sometimes hear Elvis bellowing. The nest-box was shaped like a giant stereo speaker cabinet, so being trapped inside it with the noise bouncing off the walls must have been hell. Apparently, chickens can suffer from headaches (a hunched hen with raised neck feathers is likely to have a sore head). Ours probably had migraines.

The final member of our quartet was the "Other Bantam." At this point I should confess that this bird was not the same one we'd brought home. We'd had an agitated phone call from the breeder saying that she'd accidentally sold us a bird that was part of a breeding pair and would we mind terribly swapping her for something that looked the same but wasn't? She assured us we'd never notice the difference. This was true. The replacement chicken arrived and was instantly as cowed as her predecessor.

Bossy quickly developed a particular brand of sadism for this bird, grabbing a beakful of wing and dragging her around the run, accompanied by a lot of gratifying writhing, squawking, and struggling. It was nasty and it didn't seem to get any better, but it did mean that this bird came to be known as Wimpy Chicken.

Poor Wimpy grew increasingly nervous and traumatized as the weeks went by. Jane or I coming to feed the birds appeared to be a cue for a great deal of terrified high-speed ricocheting around the run. She seemed to think that we were going to join in with the persecution, or worse.

Chickens are not feminists, and the basic problem was the lack of a rooster. An all-female hen-house can be a hotbed of bullying and viciousness, as we were fast discovering. We'd also read, or had been warned, that nature abhors an all-female flock as its extinction is guaranteed, so will sometimes "correct" this by changing the sex of one of the chickens, resulting in a he/she hen. We thought this sounded unlikely, but looked at Elvis as she bellowed "Ooo-argle-ooooooo(er)!" and wondered.

The Bird that Turned

WIMPY'S CLUTCH

Wimpy seemed to be heading for nervous collapse, and we began to feel acutely worried about her. Her life appeared to be one long nightmare. On some days she looked particularly dishevelled, with scabs on her comb after one of the others had given her a particularly nasty beaking, or mussed-about feathers as a result either of her being roughed up or trying to escape from Jane or me if we tried to hand-feed her—something Bossy, Edith and sometimes Elvis, who also indulged in some feathery histrionics, had become happy for us to do. Wimpy, however, would thunder into an uncomfortable corner, where, partially jammed in, she would panic, flap, and hurl herself against solid objects or wedge herself so completely that I'd have to extract her, something that was even more terrifying. Perhaps she'd been one of Ozzy Osbourne's bats in a previous life. That she hadn't starved to death indicated that she was at least getting some food, but we were at a loss to know what would make her existence less of a trial. By early summer, however, nature decided to resolve things.

We'd been getting a steady stream of eggs—even Wimpy dropped the odd one. One morning I found her clamped firmly to the nest, sitting on a small clutch of eggs. The look of fear had gone and there was a "Keep off they're mine" glint in her eyes. When I tried to move her she puffed up her feathers, made a strange squealing noise, and pecked the back of my hand. It didn't hurt, and it represented a sea-change in her approach to

life. Braving further pecking, I felt under her wings and discovered that she was a hot hen. Wimpy had gone broody.

There was an obvious flaw in her plan, as she could spend the next 10 years sitting on those eggs and nothing would hatch, because they weren't fertile. However, Wimpy's saving grace would turn out to be Fanny.

Fanny was a broody Marin chicken with a blood-curdling scream. We'd borrowed her from a neighbor to brood some eggs, and to accommodate Fanny we'd placed a chic tea-chest in a small, portable wire enclosure on our hen-battered lawn, and then headed off to a farm that claimed to be a professional breeder and seller of rare ducks and chickens and a supplier of fertile eggs.

APOCALYPSE NOW FARM

At the farm, tatty outbuildings gave way to large, barren fields dotted with hundreds of chicken runs in various states of disrepair. There were fenced-off areas containing stagnant patches of green water that no duck would recognize as ponds and around which depressed-looking birds congregated and shat.

Running between the enclosures and the hen-houses were dozens of asylum-seeking chickens and ducks. Some were pretty and sprightly, others moth-eaten and battered, with bald patches, red skin, and a patina of ill health.

We were accompanied by a girl of about 14, with pipe-cleaner limbs, a limp ponytail, and a distant expression. She

carried an egg carton, and when we saw a bird we liked she would open a run's nest-box and extract an egg, mark it with a felt-tip pen, and stash it in the box.

We had no particular breeds in mind, and as I lined up to pay for our haul I realized that I'd already started to forget which egg related to which bird.

I was quietly mesmerized by the shed where we paid for our clutch. It was thick with dust, stacked with crates, boxes, several broken-down incubators, and a giant, old-fashioned bird cage in which sat a bored-looking iguana, its splayed feet standing on the cage's soiled, barred floor. There was nowhere else for it to sit or sleep, nothing for it to do or look at except a procession of people carrying egg boxes.

We fled the place with a glad cry, promising never to return.

A NATURAL MOTHER

Fanny did her primitive screaming thing when we put the fertile eggs underneath her, then clamped her feathery bottom down onto them and stayed put. When Wimpy went into putative parent mode we decided to house her in the ark, and give her three of the fertile eggs, to see what would happen.

Bantams are noted for being good mothers, and Wimpy was no exception. She sat doggedly on her nest like a birdie slow cooker, stuffing her semi-naked underside (feathers are shed so that more heat reaches the eggs) against her precious trio. She

viewed our attempts to get her off the nest to feed and poop with violent distaste, and would peck and squeal whenever we went near her. She was no longer a wimpy chicken; she was a bird possessed, which is why we started calling her Psycho.

We later discovered that the nesting arrangements were less than ideal. We should have given her a swift dusting or spray of parasite-murdering chemicals, and done the same with the bedding area, which was bone dry—another mistake. Ideally there should have been a source of humidity, such as a piece of turf, grassy side uppermost and covered with straw, peat, or dry bracken, lining the nest-box.

Had Psycho been a full-sized hen we could have placed up to 12 eggs under her, but being smaller she would have consented to sit on a maximum of eight to 10 bantam eggs, which would still have been very uncomfortable. Shove too many eggs under a bird and you risk some of them being cooled, potentially killing off their contents.

Eggs can also get overheated, thanks to a combination of high summer heat and a more-than-warm mother hen. During the night, when things cool down, such eggs can actually curdle.

PSYCHO-BABIES

Nothing would have persuaded Psycho to give up her clutch, and after three weeks her perseverance paid off with two hatchlings. Meanwhile, in a moment of extreme hysteria,

Fanny had stomped two of her eggs into oblivion, nothing hatched from the third, and she went home in disgust.

Psycho continued to live up to her new name, spreading her wings like a big summer hat over the two minute balls of fluff that her flushed undercarriage had brought into the world, as she screeched and lunged at us with utter determination.

She was in her element. This was what the genes that had formed Psycho had knitted together to do, and they were going to do it properly. We watched as the two babies tottered after Psycho, who showed them how to forage and murder our lawn. If there was something particularly wonderful to eat she would cluck with the sort of unbridled enthusiasm that 1950s radio actresses employed when reading a turgid story on *Listen With Mother* ("Well, children, look at this dead slug. It's SO delicious!").

The run where we kept the new family had very fine wire mesh, which was just as well because Psycho's babies were keen to explore and, being bantams, they would have been able to squeeze through regular chicken wire, leaving them as targets for predators or to perhaps freeze to death. Chicks aren't good at handling changes in temperature, and not having instant access to a still-hot mother can quickly finish them off, or result in them maturing into weak and sickly birds.

We'd also substituted one of our normal chicken waterers for a small, pottery bottle-like thing, with a circular water trough little bigger than a dime. Fanny's owner had told us about a very weak chick she and her husband had nursed back to health over several days only to find it drowned in a full-sized waterer.

So Psycho's chicks thrived, and as they changed from fluff balls to animals with recognizable shapes and personalities we realized that neither even vaguely resembled the birds whose eggs we'd chosen. Not that it mattered. Both were bantams. One, which had the rather twee breed name of "cuckoo pekin," turned into a sort of football chicken, with delicate gray and black plumage, feathered flares, and a hard, unblinking stare. The other looked rather boring. An amorphous black nothing bird, whose shape and size vaguely resembled a seagull. She was a Belgian bearded bantam (or "barbu d'uccle porcelain," to give the bird its ghastly official name). There'd been a period after her down had fallen away when she was sadly lacking in feathers,

and we'd christened her Bald Bird, a sobriquet that was quickly reduced to "BB."

The name stuck even after she had ceased being bald and had gone on to develop a peculiar knack of changing color. Initially her feathers, legs, and beak were black. Then she molted and white feathers started to appear. Eventually she became entirely white, except for her legs and beak, which turned pink. Subsequent molts saw the reappearance of some black feathers, which dominated her plumage to a greater or lesser extent, and a black splodge appeared in her beak.

Her sister, who clearly wasn't a blood relation, was more difficult to christen. We wondered vaguely about the most inappropriate, non-obscene name we might apply to a chicken, and thought about calling her after a dangerous dog. We settled on "Satan," not because of any biblical reference, or because she was a particularly devilish animal, but because it made us laugh.

We were lucky that both were girls, but we had actually made no attempt to find out before it became obvious, largely because it's very difficult to do when they're very young and, anyway, we didn't want to know. Roosters can be hard to get rid of. We once bought a clutch of fertile eggs from a jolly lady who offered to take back any male birds. "I'll gas them for you," she said with a smile.

So we left things to nature and waited to see how the hens developed. (Bigger wattles and combs and masculine head shapes make males easier to identify after four to six weeks, although, as

we later discovered, this can be an inexact guide; you can sometimes wait much longer.) A sexing method we didn't try—because at the time we didn't know you could do it—was to startle Psycho's offspring and watch their response. One expert recommended that you throw "a hat or similar soft object over their heads and watch their reactions." Beyond the obvious "Why is this loony throwing his hat round the garden?," male birds will stand upright with their heads erect and make chirruping warning noises; female pullets will stay low and keep silent.

COMING OF AGE

During their hatless, teenaged pullet weeks, Psycho retained an iron grip on her children's activities, and even when they were very nearly as big as she was they would stuff themselves under her wings. It must have been brutally uncomfortable, but she never complained.

Nature made the decision when Psycho would no longer tolerate giving her life to birds that were now the same size as her. We knew things had changed when we heard a pained squawk. One of them had trodden on her, or exercised their until-then assumed right to eat first. Mother Dear had clearly had enough, and jabbed with her pointy little beak. The hormonal tide might have turned, but the filthy temper was still very much in place. Now, instead of using it to protect her offspring, Psycho employed it to tell them it was time to bugger off.

This didn't stop us from feeling thoroughly proud of Psycho Chicken. She was utterly brave, her offspring were well adjusted and she'd gone from the bottom of life's pecking order to the top. To say she didn't like us was an understatement, but we'd grown very fond of her, which is why we were concerned when one of her feet swelled up like a balloon and she started to limp. It seemed to happen over the course of a few hours.

This event presaged several fruitless trips to the vet and recourse to our books of chicken death. The problem turned out to be something called bumble foot, which isn't always fatal but for which there is apparently no easy cure. Perhaps she'd damaged the pad of her foot or had picked up some sort of infection from the ground.

"These things are always a bit of a mystery," said the vet. (We've since read that the problem is caused by a build-up of pus, which can apparently be leached by applying a mix of honey and Vaseline to the damaged area. Being hydrolytic, the honey naturally draws liquid towards it and can leach away the pus. Not having tried this, we can't vouch for its success.)

Either way, a course of antibiotics, squirted into a reluctant beak ("Do you think you'll be able to inject it properly?" asked the vet; oddly enough we said, "No"), didn't seem to improve matters, nor did the morning ritual of dunking the lumpy claw into an old margarine carton filled with saline water. By this stage we'd isolated Psycho in the potting shed, where she'd

continued eating, muttering and stamping about like Long John Silver, but we could see that she was getting thinner and fading.

I'm too squeamishly urban to contemplate stretching one of our chicken's necks. When I was a child I'd been given the chance to do exactly that at the factory farm, but found I couldn't. At the time I'd felt slightly embarrassed. Now I'm just glad.

"I'll chop its bleeding head off," said Keith, who runs the village garage. "That'll sort it out."

Paul, the sheep-farming partner of a near neighbor, also kept chickens and offered to do the deed ("It'll be quick") but we demurred. We realized that this was essentially selfish, and that our reluctance was based on a habit of anthropomorphizing the hens, but reasoning that it wasn't making Psycho's life any worse and that it made us feel a little better, we decided that this was an indulgence we could afford.

JUDGEMENT DAY

When the fateful morning came, we'd known for about three days that she would soon need to be dispatched. Psycho had grown listless and mopey. Under her still puffed-up feathers she was skeletal and frail.

I would get her out of the potting shed and plonk her on the lawn, where she would sit and look tired. On this particular morning she seemed especially miserable, head pulled against her chest, eyes half closed, neck feathers puffed up. Headache. I phoned

the vet, procured a cardboard box, and picked up the bird—a bag of bones covered in soft feathers. I felt upset and miserable. Ludicrously, I stopped at Satan and BB's run and proffered the sick animal to her offspring. It was the end of an era. Satan waddled over and gave her a vicious peck. They had no idea who she was.

The vet was kind. She put Psycho on the examination table. The bird had the look of the very ill, of concentrating on enduring. I decided not to watch, and sat glumly in the waiting room. "You will remember to dig a deep hole for your little friend?" said the receptionist. "You know, because of the foxes."

I'd put the cardboard box with its sad cargo in the boot of the car and was heading home when I thought, "You're 35 years old, and this is ridiculous," and then wept copiously. A small hen with a stupid name had laid some eggs, hatched some chicks, become ill, and been put to sleep. She'd probably been bonked at the farm where we'd bought her. In chicken terms she'd had a good time. As one of life's tragedies, this one came some way down the list, but this irritable bird had possessed a real strength of personality; we'd nursed her, and for Jane and me her decline had reflected experiences of equally ordinary human bereavements where bigger emotions were at stake. Time and experience had given this a different, adult resonance.

So I cried without embarrassment, went home, dug a very deep hole, buried the dead chicken, opened a bottle of red wine, and considered her replacement. I was back on familiar territory.

Lost and Found

THE WELL-TENDED GARDEN

A few weeks into chicken ownership I'd realized that I'd not only forgotten an awful lot about chicken-keeping, but had also gone through the original experience with some big knowledge gaps.

The first casualty was the lawn. Chicken shit is particularly acid. Consider the effect a sustained sparrow or blue tit guano attack can have on the paintwork of a car; remember that chickens have very productive rear ends and are also skilled scratchers, peckers, and foragers. The rapid decline of our smallish lawn shouldn't have been a surprise.

We didn't let the birds out to begin with for fear of losing them, so as we moved the ark around the garden every week or so (about 10 days being the "or so" bit), rectangular patches of yellow, defeated grass started to appear. We thought it would recover when left to its own devices and with copious applications of grass seed, but either the hens themselves or wild birds ate this, and within a year we were paying a firm of turf specialists to grub out the chicken-murdered tundra and replace it with new grass, which cost rather a lot.

We really should have shifted the run around every couple of days, which would have slowed the process down (though it wouldn't have stopped it entirely), and we did not consider the possibility that we were putting diseases into the ground that could damage our flock. Eventually, a sort of equilibrium was reached where the big chickens lived permanently in the fixed,

top run, and our two bantams, Satan and BB, were billeted in the smaller ark, which we dragged up to the vegetable patch. This could be dug over before the ark was moved, which meant that the girls' doings were mulched into the soil, and a lot of edible treats brought to the surface, which the two diminutive birds greatly enjoyed.

CHICKEN CHARM

During the spring and summer we let everyone out into the garden. This meant that the lawn escaped the concentrated dung attacks, and gave the garden a genuinely rustic charm. There's something very restful about the noise made by contented chickens as they amble about and forage, and the colors and movement of the birds do add to the look of a garden.

On summer evenings we would take a couple of glasses of wine and sit on a bench and watch our ladies getting on with being chickens; we were entertained when less shy birds, such as Mrs. Brown (one of our subsequent purchases) or Satan, would trundle up to us for some attention, or better still some food.

It didn't take much in the way of an edible bribe to persuade them to sit on the bench with us. Satan in particular thought laps made decent roosting places, and, if she had nothing better to do, was quite happy to sit and be fussed over. Occasionally, after prolonged tickling behind her shoulder blades she would close her bulging eyes and fall asleep.

The downside to this was the gradual destruction wreaked on the flower-beds, plants, and vegetables. Dust baths would appear where bulbs had been planted. Annuals would be dug in by Jane, then dug out, stripped, and dumped by Elvis. An entire crop of broad beans became instant chicken snack food. Not being a natural gardener, it took me a while to notice the craters and withered roots, but Jane's cries of "Get off!" and "Don't sit on that!" or "Martin, look what your bloody hens have done to my tulips," soon alerted me to what was going on. That the birds became my exclusive property when they were being pains wasn't a surprise.

Protecting flower-bed edges and borders with lightweight 18-inch high garden netting is said to be a good way of discouraging the vandalism, although I suspect it would only be a matter of time before such defenses would be breached.

Jane eventually began lobbying for permanent imprisonment. I resisted, partly, I'm ashamed to say, because I was mostly working from home and the hens came to visit me. Being tucked away from the rest of the world for hours at a stretch in a converted garden building, which operated as an office, meant that I often appreciated the company.

Once, having left the door of the shed open and gone into the house for lunch, I returned and was amused to discover a warm, newly laid egg nestling in my in-tray. So, I found an old cat box, filled it with straw, and put it in the corner of my office.

Soon, I was being entertained by a procession of birds using the cat box to divest themselves of their eggs. Each felt it was their personal territory, and there was much angst if, say, Satan found Egghead—another recent arrival—in "her" box.

When the door was open the birds would waddle in, and sometimes made rather a lot of noise as every pelvic muscle was given a thorough work over to pop another egg into the world.

Mrs. Brown, who produced hand-grenade-sized eggs, did a particularly good line in agonized moaning, as she hunkered down, pushed like mad, and picked up pieces of straw with her beak and chucked them over her shoulder.

TELEPHONE ETIQUETTE

When I was on the phone interviewing some car industry executive the sound effects were sometimes hard to explain. This was certainly true when I managed to get an interview with the now largely forgotten Labour Party paymaster general, Geoffrey Robinson, who bit the political bullet after loaning ex-Northern Ireland secretary Peter Mandelson some cash to buy a very large London house.

Robinson was in the process of being given a pasting by a House of Commons Select Committee, and it was well known that he was finishing a biography in which he put the boot in to all manner of political grandees of the day, including Tony Blair. Oddly enough, Robinson wasn't the most approachable public figure when it came to being interviewed by journalists.

So when he called me I had something of a scoop. Before smugness causes my head to explode, it should be mentioned that our Geoff had been a car industry executive in the 1970s, and I wanted to know about the highly newsworthy, controversial story of, er, his time running British Leyland's Italian subsidiary, making left-hand drive Minis. At the time, any

hack getting this man to speak on the record about anything wasn't doing too badly. He was even paying for the call.

Anyway, about 10 minutes into a conversation about what it was like getting Italians to make Minis, BB the chicken decided to visit my office. She was a demanding guest. If you did not pay her instant attention, she made a lot of noise for a long time. This is exactly what happened.

"So, what changes did you make to the Mini for the Italian market?" I fearlessly asked.

"Ark! Ark! Ark! Ark! Ark!" screeched BB.

"Pardon?" said Geoffrey Robinson.

"I said. . . ."

"Ark! Ark! Ark! Ark!"

"What CHANGES did YOU MAKE to the MINI?"

"Aaaark! Aaaark!"

"For the ITALIAN. . ."

"Arka! Arka! Arka ARKA!!!"

"I'm sorry I still can't quite hear you. . ."

"THE ITALIAN MARKET!"

As Geoffrey Robinson explained what he had done to sell Minis to a nation of baby Fiat lovers (added reversing lights, you'll be thrilled to hear) I gathered up the protesting BB, turfed her outside, banged the door shut, and carried on the interview. Geoffrey Robinson never asked what the noise was and I didn't try to explain.

BB'S REVENGE

When the interview was finished BB was nowhere to seen, or indeed heard. This wasn't unusual, and I imagined that she was sulking under a bush, but when she didn't appear for supper we began to worry, and searched the garden. No chicken. We scoured our neighbors' plots, but found nothing. It was winter and grew dark early. Her sister Satan took to her perch alone for the first time. We did not fancy BB's chances of survival. She was slow, and her plumage at the time was virtually all white. Easy prey for a fox, badger, or even a dog. Two days later we had given up hope, and imagined that if we found anything it would be a scattering of white feathers. Then I thought I heard a scratching noise behind the freezer in the kitchen.

Had I left the back door open? Had the little tyke got into the house and wedged herself behind the freezer? It was impossible to move the freezer or shine a torch behind it to see what was going on.

"Do we have any tinned sweetcorn?" I asked.

"No," said Jane.

I decided to go out and buy some. It was 8:30 on a weekday evening, and the journey involved a five-mile trip.

"Would you like to go across the road and get our chicken?" said Jane when I got back.

We never found out what the scratching noise was, although it could have been the couple next door engaging in some

kitchen DIY, but while I'd been out another neighbor had knocked and asked if we were the owners of a small white hen.

Having been banished from my office, BB had had a birdie fit and managed to squeeze under the gate that divided our garden from the person whose boyfriend was Paul the Shepherd.

Exactly what happened next is conjecture, but two of his sheepdogs were in their garden, and they probably found BB very interesting. She managed to evade them, but in the process crossed the road—I know, "Why did she do that?" Whatever, it was another lucky escape, and she found herself in the garden of the family who lived across the way. For the next couple of days BB had avoided being eaten (a small miracle, given her coloring), and was discovered early one morning by one of our neighbor's children, who'd imprisoned her in a rabbit hutch and expressed the hope that they might be able to keep her. As I collected the thinner, but otherwise unharmed bird I was happy to promise unlimited visiting rights.

Satan greeted her wandering sister with a few grumpy clucks, and if it's possible for a chicken to look chastened, this one did. BB was certainly a lot quieter, and for the next few weeks seemed disinclined to leave her run.

In the meantime I scoured the garden fences in search of holes through which a chicken might squeeze, and attached some wire to the bottom of the gate to prevent further escapes.

WAIFS AND STRAYS

Usually we seem to have a penchant for finding lost or dumped animals, rather than mislaying them ourselves, and mostly they've been dogs.

The first was a miserable Heinz 57-style puppy that had been abandoned near a big municipal park near where Jane was living in Ilford. We knew the dog had been dumped because we could still see the imprint in his fur where the collar had been.

We took the depressed animal to the local police station. The slack-jawed man behind the desk, who clearly didn't want this sad bundle piddling on his patch, said it would go to Battersea Dogs' Home and lied about how they put strays to sleep if they weren't claimed "in a week." We called his bluff and told an animal-loving neighbor about our find.

She was a redoubtable East Londoner with connections to the provisional wing of an unofficial Essex animal-lovers collective. Soon she and a group of not-to-be-messed-with ladies swooped on the police station, liberated the dog, and found it a home within the week.

One winter's evening we rescued two Staffordshire bull terriers that were running around in the middle of the road in an Essex village. Again, neither had collars, and both were terrified. This was something we discovered when I stopped the car, opened the door, and these powerful dogs hurled themselves inside. One cringed in the footwell behind the back seat, the

other subsided gratefully on Jane's lap and shoved his squashed-looking face into her cleavage.

Relieved that these dogs were interested in us as protectors rather than as comestibles, we tried to find their owners. I tried a pub that was close by.

"Could belong to Joe," said a gnarled-looking man in a bobble hat.

Apparently, Joe had two Staffordshires, lived in a cottage near the pub, had separated from his wife, and grown fond of the bottle as a result. The dogs had got out more than once according to our informant.

I went up to the front of the cottage. It was dark and foggy, and there was no obvious sign of a front door. As I tottered into what looked like the front garden a downstairs light was switched on, revealing a sink around which a lot of dirty crockery was piled.

The exact sequence of events that followed is a little hazy, but the next thing I noticed was a naked female foot being gingerly lowered into the sink. Then its owner saw me—a strange man standing in her garden. The foot was speedily withdrawn and two faces, a man's and a woman's, were pressed against the window. They were squinting at me, and not in a welcoming way.

I hopped about in that "I'm-a-harmless-twit-not-a-serial-killer" mode Englishmen have when confronted with a situation like this, and after some mutual, inconclusive

mouthing along the lines of "What do you want?," "Er, do you own any dogs?," the window was opened and a rather stilted conversation took place. I discovered that the cottage was semi-detached and that they were the neighbors of the dog owner, who was out rather than pissed, and that his dogs were fine and staying with the ex-wife.

As for the foot in the sink, a medically related explanation was offered (which time has expunged from my mind), and the three of us parted on friendly terms. This did not, however, solve the dog problem.

Back in the pub Bobble Hat Man was sanguine.

"Dog catcher lives at the top of the village. Tell you what, I'll drive up there and you follow me in your car," he said.

So I headed back to the car. (As you imagine my doing so, you might wonder what any of this has to do with chickens. Well, stick with me and all will be revealed.)

By this time the car's interior had steamed up nicely, and the night was punctuated by regular woofings, yappings, yelpings, and pantings. Inside, Jane was slobbered on but otherwise much as before.

One dog was still in full-on cringe mode on the floor, the other was half on her lap but had somehow managed to get its arse partially wedged against the end of the handbrake. As I maneuvered its buttocks a car horn sounded and Bobble Hat Man trundled by in an elderly Metro.

Having been detached from the handbrake, the dog decided it wanted to sit on both of us. I had the rear end, Jane had the front. This meant that having got the car into first gear I couldn't select second, because the dog was in the way.

Not wishing to lose the man with the hat, I made slow, engine-screaming progress up the hill after him.

He was waiting for us outside a neat council house, along with a chunky man with what looked like a giant butterfly net. This man spoke kindly to the dogs and moved swiftly, netting each of them, pulling them from our car, and depositing them in the back of a van.

"Strange that people dump animals like this. They both look well cared for, but I think that's what's happened. Still, shouldn't have a problem getting them re-housed," he said.

THE CHICKEN THAT CROSSED THE ROAD

Since then, more canine waifs have emerged from ditches as we've been driving past (Tonsil the Irish wolfhound) or turned up in our front garden (Rollo, a mongrel), but they always had homes to go to. We wanted a dog, but decided to wait until one found us, which is how we now own Hoover, a crossbred terrier, who was discovered by the side of the road on our way back from a garden center.

So perhaps we shouldn't have been surprised that the only other lost animal to come into our lives was a chicken.

I was taking the car for its annual inspection when the bird ran in front of me and narrowly avoided getting squashed. It was a pure-bred bantam Silkie, with the feathers on its head looking rather like a madly permed busby hat, and the rest of the plumage resembling a feather boa.

I stopped the car and gave chase. The bird had shot through a gap in a hedge which separated the grounds of what had been the local manor house from the rest of the village. I was on nodding terms with the owners and did not think they would have me shot as a trespasser, so I squeezed in after the hen.

It was November and dank, and I was in a hurry, but I assumed that the bird was somebody's pet and that it would be missed. In front of me was a large pile of garden rubbish, which was clearly intended as a bonfire, and I moved slowly round this because I could hear some agitated clucking noises.

Then I saw the chicken. We engaged in a fruitless, silent-movie-style chase round and round the large obstacle course. Eventually the bird tried to burrow inside the pile of rubbish, a process made difficult by a tangle of spiky bramble-bush cuttings. These slowed down its escape, but also meant that I could lunge at the hen and catch it. As my hand drew nearer to the frantic animal it finally managed to wriggle past the sharp branches and into the soft leaves beyond them. Short of dismantling someone else's bonfire I wasn't going to be able to lay hands on it. Reluctantly I gave up, reasoning that it was unlikely anybody was going to put a match to its sodden hiding place, certainly in the short term, and at least the chicken was away from the road.

THE LAUGHING CAVALIER

A couple of days later I mentioned this encounter to a man known in our household as the Laughing Cavalier, thanks to his rather fine pointy beard, and a face which, in repose, looked anything but cheerful. On the surface he was a slightly lugubrious 50-something, pathos in dungaree overalls, but there was also an interesting-bloke twinkle about him.

The best way to describe the Cavalier would be as a Renaissance odd-jobs man. He'd travelled, he'd had all sorts of surprising careers and career changes, and seemed happy to live life on his own terms. This meant an apparently singular existence in a big, permanent trailer, tucked away among some farm buildings in private woodland, not far from the grounds of the big house where the Silkie had taken refuge.

He drove an ancient Peugeot hatchback, from which he had removed the front passenger seat to accommodate the tins of paint, tools, sections of timber, and bits of scaffolding tower he employed to earn a living.

The Cavalier's approach to work was that of an artisan. Whether he was repairing the clapboarding of one of the distinctive wooden houses found in the part of Kent where we lived, or resuscitating apparently knackered sections of cast-iron drainpipe with ingenious applications of drain off-cuts and mastic, progress was always glacial. We'd got to know him because he'd been working on the house next to ours. Scaffolding would be erected, paint scraped, and then he would vanish. A week or so might pass and he would reappear, clutching a blowtorch and a fresh paint-removing implement. This process went on for several months. Eventually he became such a familiar presence that when I escaped my word-processor toil to make yet more tea, I'd generally make him a cup too.

It was during one of these tea-breaks that I mentioned the elusive chicken.

"Oh, I've seen that several times," said the Cavalier. "Beats me why it hasn't been eaten by a fox."

There were plenty of fox paths in the wood and the bird apparently hadn't had much success at being inconspicuous.

"Why don't we catch it?" I suggested. The Cavalier didn't seem massively enthused by the idea, but eventually agreed, "When I go home for lunch."

Finding the hen didn't take long. It was scratching around in a dip among some decayed leaves and on seeing us coming scuttled into a tangle of weeds and bushes. The Cavalier and I encircled this, closed in, and lunged ineptly. With a squawk and much flapping the small, black chicken shot past us and back into the clearing. We soon discovered that it was easier to move quickly along a woodland floor if you were a tiny hen rather than a normal-sized human being. The ground is uneven, soft in places, hard in others, and invariably slippery.

Making curious, pincer-like scooping gestures with our hands, the Cavalier and I slipped and slithered about after the Silkie in a chase that involved bursts of running-around punctuated by breathless creeping about by some bush or thicket into which the animal had scuttled.

When we chased the bird into the open it would appear to tire occasionally, but always managed to put on a flapping

spurt of speed when one of us lunged for it. However, it did seem to be slowing down, so we persevered.

It was clear that the Cavalier was better at chicken-catching than me, and was also less worried about what the chase might do to his clothes. He was out of breath and frankly exasperated by the whole business when the tiny bird did its trick of doubling back and running past him, so he executed a kind of domestic fowl rugby tackle, landing sideways in a pile of decomposing leaves. When he stood up, he was clasping an unhappy, wriggling bird.

Panting, he said, "It's yours, I don't want it," before handing me a slightly skinny and rather soiled, wet chicken, then adding something about there being enough meat on the bird to make a decent dinner.

SAMSON AND DELILAH

At home we'd been given a small wire enclosure and I'd made a lockable nest-box for birds that were either broody or ill, and this was where our new arrival was placed. She seemed subdued and was only mildly interested in the food and drink proffered to her. The other chickens were in the garden, and they soon stomped up to the enclosure and began menacing its occupant. Egghead in particular began trying to peck the Silkie through the wire mesh, causing her to retreat into the nest-box and hide.

I'd hoped being somewhere dry and safe would make the bird perk up, but it didn't seem to. Instead she remained moribund and quiet, so I began to make inquiries in the village. Had anyone lost a chicken?

Mac, the village's workaholic baker and shopkeeper suggested that I ask a local matriarch whose family had lived there for generations. She knew everybody and kept chickens.

I'd met this formidable lady at a local bring-and-buy sale, where I discovered that she was a great-grandmother and had the natural authority you would expect this standing to confer. She'd also taken to calling me "mate."

So when I knocked on the door of her house I felt a little nervous. This lady was a force of nature who did not suffer fools. With my plummy vowels and soft, white-collar work, I suspected that I might fall into the fool category as far as she was concerned. So when it was clear that she was out and I only had to leave a message, the coward in me breathed a sigh of relief.

An hour later the phone rang and a purposeful female voice said, "Hello, Martin. Got your message." It was the great-grandmother who knew everyone. The chicken wasn't hers but she did know the owner, another lady who would be thrilled to know the animal was safe. It was only later that I realized that I was no longer "mate," and that the matriarch lady had used my Christian name for the first time. Events had allowed me to cross an unspoken threshold, which meant I had moved from being

somebody who perhaps didn't know what was what, to being OK really. This was an unexpected bonus of chicken rescuing.

Another bonus came when Jane and I took the bird home, using the old cat box.

"Home" was a run in the garden of a very pretty cottage in the middle of the village. Her owner was a middle-aged lady we'd been on nodding terms with for a while in a sharing-the-line-at-the-Post-Office kind of way, and she beamed with pleasure when we arrived.

This occasioned much excited scrabbling from the cat box. Its cargo had up to then been silent, wary, and rather depressed-looking, but as soon as she recognized her surroundings the bird perked up enormously.

We discovered that the hen was called Delilah and that she lived with a rooster who, naturally enough, was christened Samson. If Delilah was pleased to see her owner, then Samson was ecstatic when he saw Delilah. There was much mutual flapping and clucking, even before the joyful reunion. Both birds rushed to greet each other, and Samson did a little war dance, circling his beloved. It was actually quite touching.

It turned out that during the day Samson and Delilah had the run of their owner's garden and Delilah must have found a gap in the hedge. The owner had gone through the usual process of searching fruitlessly, and after more than a week had assumed that Delilah had become something else's snack.

But Delilah survived to go on and do the parental thing. The following summer she went broody and sat on a clutch of quails' eggs. The result was a skittering collection of minute baby birds, swarming round a clucking, pom-pom-headed foster parent who looked nothing like them.

By all accounts Delilah was thoroughly conscientious about her tiny chargelings. Her owner said that she'd always had a real aptitude as a mother and, although you might be reaching for the sick bag at this point, this made her rescue seem particularly worthwhile. Even the Laughing Cavalier managed an ever-so-slightly soulful smile when told of her progress.

HEN-SITTING

These events made us regularly check our own garden for possible new hen escape routes, but one thing we hadn't considered was how our own birds would be looked after if we went away. Again we struck lucky.

Our good fortune started with the sound of a chicken we didn't recognize. Sad though it may seem, you do get to tell which bird is which by the sounds made by individuals. Mrs. Brown sounds plaintive, even when she's being vile; Elvis sounds worried; Egghead makes a staccato cluck, redolent of a fussy machine-gun.

"Ooooaaaark," went the hen we didn't recognize.

"Weeeeooooo," came the response.

"Which one of them is that?" asked Jane.

It turned out that the noise was being made by a very capable chicken-impersonator called Jack.

Jack and Eileen are a retired couple who live at the end of the terrace that was our home when the chickens first came into

our lives. Part of their garden backed onto ours, and Jack would secretly commune with the birds.

It turned out that Jack's father had kept hens, and he took a great interest in ours. Jack and his wife have a fabulous garden, and we were soon being offered vegetable roots and other delicacies, which the girls loved.

Eventually we asked whether Jack and Eileen might be prepared to look after the birds when we went on holiday, in exchange for eggs.

It was a brilliant deal for the hens and for us. Jack had clearly acquired his dad's chicken-husbandry skills, and we'd come back to find the hens looking happy and contented, often with some vegetable treat hanging from a piece of twine in their run.

Had this willing, kind chicken-sitting not been so readily available I'm not sure what we would have done, and it wasn't something we'd considered when rushing off to buy the birds. Perhaps we would have advertised in the local shop: "Wanted, hen-sitter. Must have own Wellington boots and good sense of humor," or something like that, but having people we knew overseeing the chickens when we couldn't, did make a big difference to our peace of mind. If disaster had struck, a mistake been made or had somebody—hen-sitter or hen—keeled over in our absence, the potential for awkwardness and misunderstanding was much reduced.

To date, only one bird has chosen to wait until we were on holiday before sliding from her perch and making for the celestial allotment. Jack dealt with this unhappy episode and almost apologized that her demise took place on his watch.

Our luck held chicken-sitting-wise after we moved house. Some discreet inquires brought us into contact with Robert, a 14-year-old Scout who had to carry out some "good works" to win his Duke of Edinburgh medal.

For a very reasonable fee, Robert, a bloke of few words when dealing with a Cro-Magnon era old fart like me, but someone who does a very good line in explanatory nodding, would feed and water our feathered crew. Any eggs laid would be his. I've no idea what Prince Philip thinks of the youth of today ("Rankin' cool mothers, who should bloody well have less dissing!" or something. No, let's scrub that: the grumpy stereotype is much more amusing), but this particular youth took his work above and beyond the call of duty. He looked after the birds' culinary needs and even cleaned them out. We didn't ask him to do this, and some sociologists might worry about a teenager who voluntarily cleans up the bedrooms not of other people but of other species, but all we can say is, "Phil, give the boy a medal."

In Sickness and in Health

RED MITE STRIKES

Although we've so far managed to avoid inept beheading, Jane and I have visited a number of accidental cruelties on the hens. The biggest is related to the nest-box I built for them and something called red mite.

I'd carefully enveloped the outside of the nest-box with roofing felt, which was nailed into position. This certainly kept the water out, but meant that there were gaps between felt and woodwork. When the summer came these gaps became a home for red mites. These are tiny bloodsucking creatures. They live in hen-house cracks and crevices, coming out at night for a good suck, and can give the birds anemia. They like human blood, too, as we discovered.

The first indication that something was wrong was when Bossy and co. started to try sleeping outside. I just thought this was some summer-related thing and foolishly forced them into the hen-house and shut the door. After a couple of nights of this I began to feel a bit itchy. By this stage the infestation had well and truly taken hold.

One night I shone a torch into the bedding area and became aware of a prickling sensation on the back of my hand. I looked down and saw it was crawling with tiny red dots. Others were jumping after them. The walls of the hen-house were similarly encrusted, and so were the birds' feathers. I had been forcing the hens to live with this.

I plunged open the door and retreated. By this stage the red mites had made friends with my scalp. I showered hastily and the next day we sought advice. We were told that red mites like a combination of hot weather and dirty conditions. I had not been as diligent as I should have been in changing the bedding, and this was the result.

We had to spray all our hens with tick repellent, a process that involved holding them upside down by the feet, where they would flap and protest as I squirted them with evil-smelling fluid.

Next on the agenda was the hen-house itself. We moved the birds into a temporary run. I went to a farm shop and bought some specialist insecticide, which, when mixed with water, also stank horribly. I poured the concoction into a garden bug sprayer and, kitted out in disposable paper overalls, face mask, and stylish shower cap, did battle with the red menace.

This was a prolonged, revolting process, but no more than I deserved, and it never seemed entirely successful. Eventually a neighbor told us to move the hens out for 72 hours and blitz the hen-house interior with creosote. This did the trick. Hundreds of mites bubbled out of corners and crevices.

When we moved house, I built a new hen-house with better ventilation, a lot less felt covering, and fewer places for the vile creatures to live and breed. We still spray the birds two or three times in the summer and, so far, the problem hasn't come back.

I also clean the hens out at least once a week, laying sheets of cardboard on the hen-house floor and nesting area, which can be removed and rolled up (you can also buy ready-made hen-houses with removable floors, which can be cleaned). The cardboard can be unravelled and staked out in the garden with bamboo poles, becoming a sort of card, sawdust, and chicken crud wafer sandwich, which eventually rots down and makes great compost.

Hens also suffer from other mites and ticks. Feather loss and sore-looking red patches of skin around the chest and wing tips are a giveaway. These sores can sometimes require regular applications of Vaseline, a process that is rarely enjoyed by either hen or owner.

THE IMPORTANCE OF HANDLING

Comical though it may sound, regular handling is also important. The birds will protest, and some will give the impression that they're convinced you're about to ram a nuclear warhead up their egg holes, but the hysteria will often decrease with familiarity, and if you're having to give regular attention to a particular bird the less stressed it is the better. Some will become very tame, which is endearing and helpful.

On balance, if it's a choice between being tickled by a human being or grubbing up that human's vegetable patch in search of worms and wriggly wildlife, then your advances are unlikely to be warmly received, but if you have food and/or

there's nothing better to do, then it's quite possible to have some birdie one-on-one.

Some of ours enjoy being planted on a lap and having attention paid to them. Wearing old clothing is important here, as chickens cannot be house-trained.

Hens like a good massage from the shoulder blades to the tail, although it must be said that some birds get a cheap thrill from this and will squat obviously and expectantly. If you have a reasonably high embarrassment threshold and like giving pleasure to others, then this is not a problem.

In a non-pervy sense, making friends with your chickens will allow you to check for rattling breath (a sign of respiratory trouble), nasty discharges, and something called "scaly leg"—a self-explanatory problem brought on by tiny mites which get behind the bird's leg scales; the mites can cause swelling and in serious cases result in the birds losing toes; soft-feather breeds, such as Silkies, are more inclined to suffer from this. Prevention involves regular cleaning of the hens' run and bedding area, and disinfecting it every so often. The cure, which can take anything up to a year, involves getting a jam jar, filling it with surgical spirit, and dunking a leg in it for 20 seconds. According to the redoubtable *Poultry and Waterfowl Problems*, you do one leg then the other, before repeating the process. Vets can also inject a mite repellent.

Handling birds is a good way to make sure nobody is starving to death.

Very thin birds are skilled at concealing their state, and it's often possible to find that an outwardly healthy-looking hen is actually pathetically thin.

This happened to Satan. One morning I noticed that she was pecking in mid-air, picked her up, and found that she felt delicate and incredibly skinny. She'd contracted a respiratory problem that had caused the tubes behind her eyes to inflame so that she could no longer focus properly. A serious shot of antibiotics and a day's hand-feeding seemed to bode well. She started to eat unaided, but 48 hours later couldn't even stand up. She had been our very first hatchling and had a great character. When we lost her the degree of sadness Jane and I felt surprised both of us, since we naively believed that as by-now old hands at dealing with birds that turned up their claws we'd be inured when this one went.

Satan had been heading for her fourth birthday, quite old for a chicken, and they do simply pack up and die, but I did wonder whether this would have happened if I'd been more diligent.

Watching the hens eat can be entertaining, but, given their predilection for bullying, it's also a good way to see if anyone is being prevented from getting to the feed. Sometimes a bird will need to be isolated and given regular feeding, and, if it's very weak, being put in a dry, comfortable environment can make a lot of difference. If the animal doesn't drop dead and appears to get better it's worth keeping it apart from the others for a few more days to really build up its strength, and when it is

reintroduced keep a watchful eye for the bullying that caused the problem to start with.

TOE BALLS

Toe balls are another perennial problem. They are basically hardened clumps of mud and crud that attach themselves to a chicken's feet like filthy necklace beads. They make foraging and perching difficult, and can get so big that birds can sometimes break their toes.

A great way to give hens toe balls is to be lax about changing their bedding. Chickens like to roost in one spot. This results in a concentration of excrement in which they will happily stand and squelch around. This crap is the glue that binds toe ball to bird. Getting rid of toe balls means sticking a bird's feet in a bucket of water to soften them, then gently breaking the balls up and prying them off. This can be time-consuming, stressful for the hen, and uncomfortable for you, especially if the result is a face full of flapping wing. Care has to be taken to avoid damaging toes as you yank at the turd excrescences. Sometimes the balls might need attacking with a pair of scissors, but, for obvious reasons, be careful how you cut.

Satan suffered a broken toe because of one of these things, and became an amputee as a result. The vet said her now useless digit would have to come off and added that a general anesthetic was needed, something that bird respiratory systems aren't always good at dealing with. Satan stood a fair chance of dying, so would

I mind terribly signing a disclaimer promising not to sue if this happened? Imagining some creepy "no win, no fee" solicitor trying to screw money from the vet for "distress and reduction in earnings caused due to loss of bantam chicken," I was happy to sign, and happier still when I phoned after the operation and could hear a series of loud, disgruntled squawks as the receptionist told me that Satan ("Is she really called that?") was now minus a toe but otherwise fine. This loss didn't seem to bother the bird at all. The nub healed and quickly became invisible, and her capacity to perch and run with an extraordinary sideways bounce from one foot to the other seemed unimpaired. I did, however, keep an eye on her feet after that.

EGG-BOUND CHICKENS

We became a bit concerned when red streaks began appearing on Bald Bird's tiny white eggs. They resembled bloody skid marks, and were a problem brought about by muscle strain when she was laying, which we cured by feeding her lumps of bread dunked in cod liver oil. Apparently chickens can become egg-bound: it's a form of cramp, and if you see an egg protruding but apparently stuck the remedy will necessitate you applying some olive oil or Vaseline to the birdie butt. Tamer birds can have their backsides blasted with a hairdryer (thank you again *Poultry and Waterfowl Problems*) or dangled over a pan of hot water—both delightful tasks for everyone concerned. Alternatively, the animal

can be put in a well-ventilated cardboard box and placed near a radiator. Generally, nature will take its course after a bit.

I could go on to talk about cannibalism, prolapse, and heart problems, but won't. Many hen disasters relate to passive or active neglect, how well the birds are housed, how clean they are, and whether they have stress-free lives. This last point is often connected to the previous ones.

RATTED

Rats complete our catalogue of horrors. Both the houses where we've kept chickens backed on to fields where rats live, and

when the fields are plowed up these animals tend to travel farther to feed and nest.

The best way to discourage rats is to keep the feed in a dry, secure, gnaw-proof place. We use a metal dustbin (rats can chew through plastic ones if they're hungry enough), but that didn't stop them from nesting under the shed next to our original chicken run, and then burrowing into the birds' territory. We saw the tunnels first, then the tunnellers nonchalantly squatting next to the apparently unconcerned chickens and helping themselves to whatever food was available.

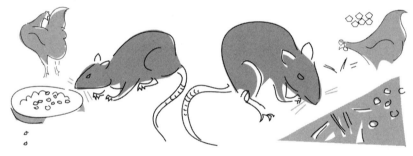

Rats are bright and determined, and when their regular territory is disturbed they are quite happy to move in on yours. I spent a slimy weekend digging out the run, surrounding my excavations with chicken wire and old bricks, then covering this with soil. It took the rats less than 24 hours to dig under these defenses. We set traps, which were studiously ignored, and noticed with alarm that the rats had started trying to chew their way into the hen-house itself. We'd heard stories of hens having

toes and even feet bitten away by hungry rats, and there was the potential for our eggs to be trashed and stolen.

Scattering food encourages rats, especially if the weather turns nasty as the food gets damp and mulchy and the chickens disdainfully refuse to eat it. Rats have no such scruples and will happily engorge anything you leave out.

I called the local Environmental Health Department (aka the exterminators), and was pleasantly surprised to discover that the service was free since we lived in a rural area. We also told the neighbors about the problem and what we were doing about it. Since one of them had a small child and kept guinea pigs this seemed to be a tactful thing to do. Everyone was understanding ("We live in the country" seemed to be the response), but might have been less so if we'd said nothing and they'd met one of our unwanted extended family.

TERMINATOR

I wasn't looking forward to meeting the exterminator. I'd previously encountered two local-authority wasp-murderers. One had an emaciated moustache and told us in tedious detail about the alleged infidelities of a local pub owner's wife whom we knew slightly. We nodded sagely but inwardly cheered as he told us the woman had banned his friend for unsuccessfully trying to whip a tablecloth out from under a full pint glass, which, fairly obviously, smashed.

The other bloke sounded like a posh Leonard Cohen, and said of his calling: "Oh, I'll kill anything for money."

The rat dispatcher was a man of indeterminate years— basically 18–30—with a falsetto voice, who perked up as soon as he saw our hens.

"Used to keep a few birds," he said blithely. It turned out a few meant a couple of hundred, and he was an endless font of knowledge and enthusiasm about breeds and chicken husbandry. He applied bait in the form of grain dyed a nasty blue color, and said that the rats would soon learn that this was an unhealthy place for them to be. "We'll get rid of them, but they'll come back from time to time," he said cheerfully.

That was how it proved, but when they did occasionally appear (usually after a harvest) we'd call the exterminator, make him a cup of tea, he'd do his rat bumping-off stuff, then offer us advice on ways to look after our birds.

You've probably read this chapter and thought, "Oh God, death, disease, and vermin," but bear in mind that once we moved house and I built a chicken run in a less hidden but still sheltered spot and bought a metal dustbin for the chicken food, the rats ceased to be a problem. You stand as much chance of having rodent visitors by keeping rabbits or guinea pigs. I haven't found either to be as interesting as pets and neither lay eggs, although I suppose they are edible—guinea-pig fricassee, anyone?

Confused of Kent

SHE WAS A HE

Our first rooster was an accident called Yvette.

We'd been given a clutch of fertile, fist-sized eggs from what were described as French-style free-range farm chickens. Mrs. Brown's laying habits had become erratic and it seemed sensible to have at least one bird who was going to be regularly productive, and rearing it ourselves would be fun.

Satan had decided to become broody, so we stuffed four of these boulderesque offerings under her wings and after 21 days they produced three very healthy, very fluffy chicks.

Their presence strained relations between BB and Satan. No longer did they get along peaceably. Satan, who was the more strident of the two, now viewed her sister as a potential obstacle to her offspring's development, and would go for her if she tried to get to food before they did.

BB clearly resented this and would sneak up on the sainted babies and give them a vicious peck when she thought their mother wasn't looking. Quite often she would miscalculate here. The result would be a few seconds of total war as Satan meted out instant justice.

As they matured, our trio all seemed to be girls. Two had light-colored plumage, the third more distinctive darker feathers. We decided to keep this bird and gave the other two away.

Now christened Yvette, she matured quickly, if not especially prettily, and was soon towering over her mother and BB. Satan's

maternal instincts had long since shut down, and both she and BB clearly found Yvette an irksome companion.

Yvette was more than clumsy: she was a dyspraxic chicken, with an endless capacity to cannon into water containers or stamp ineptly on food bowls so that they were up-ended and covered the food. The older birds reacted to this by pecking her regularly and viciously, sending Yvette into paroxysms of nerves, causing her to run around at high speed and once again crash into things, like the upturned food containers and the only slightly flexible wire fencing.

When I had to pick her up, Yvette would plumb new depths of terror, and I began to worry that she was going to injure herself. When she started to limp I wasn't surprised, and I put the bird in a separate run hoping this would reduce the stress. It didn't, and after about a week she could barely stand up. A trip to the vet was arranged.

"Can't see anything obviously wrong with this one. She might have pulled a muscle, damaged a tendon or something," said the vet, reaching for $45 worth of steroids and a syringe.

I was given a large bottle of "wide-spectrum antibiotic." This basically means it can be force fed to everything from bantams to beagles and wipe out a variety of ailments—or not.

Yvette showed no signs of improvement. She was by now completely immobile, which at least meant that she couldn't escape from me when I came to give her a daily squirt of

medicine. To do this I would tuck her under one arm to clamp her wings and stop her wriggling ("OOOOOAAAAGH!!! SQUAWK! SQUAWK! EEEEEEOOOOOAAAGH!!!" etc), pinch open her beak with a thumb and forefinger (time for much head rolling and neck jerking), before managing to position the needle-less plastic syringe and spurt antibiotic into the terrified patient's pecking gear. Sometimes she would wrench her head free and I would accidentally squirt the medicine in her eye, which meant loading up the syringe and repeating the stressful process.

At this point I was usually working from home, but occasionally my job took me to the editorial office of a trade magazine for car dealers, where I would reconstitute press releases about brake linings and men in suits getting new jobs. On these days I wore half-decent clothes, on which Yvette would sometimes poop wetly. That it was 6:30 in the morning heightened the joy of these encounters—and yes, it was my fault for wearing work clothes for animal husbandry in the first place.

Yvette did not appear to be getting better. After a couple of weeks sitting on itchy straw and in her own excrement she was looking sore, matted and unhappy, and had taken to stretching her neck on the ground and trying to pull herself forward with her beak. It looked pitiful.

The only thing that gave her pleasure was food. She always ate with undisguised greed. Despite this we decided reluctantly

that the bird was starting to suffer, and that our motives for keeping her alive were selfish. I asked the vet to prepare a lethal injection and set off for the surgery with Yvette imprisoned in a cardboard box. The bird was sitting on the examination table and the vet was holding the syringe when something odd happened. Yvette began wildly flapping her wings, and half standing she staggered forward and propelled herself back to the safety of the cardboard box. It was the first time she'd moved in weeks.

"That chicken has spirit," said the vet. "I think you should give it another chance."

PERSONAL TRAINER

Which is how I became an amateur hen physiotherapist. I took the reprieved Yvette home and considered ways of getting her back on her feet and, in a very real sense, out of the shit.

My office was a building in the back garden, so I laid some newspaper on the floor next to my desk and plonked the reluctant patient next to me. She was rather stinky and clearly didn't appreciate the company, but couldn't get away. Food and water were put near her, and in between writing I would try standing her up.

She would sway uncertainly, try and support her still rapidly increasing bulk with her wings, fail and fall over, sometimes half into her tin water bowl, splashing my desk and trouser bottoms in the process.

This was clearly an unsatisfactory arrangement for both of us, but then inspiration struck. I got a ball of string, took a pair of scissors to an old shirt, and made a sort of chicken cradle-cum-baby bouncer. Getting Yvette into this proved difficult. She

made a lot of "I knew it, you're going to kill me!" noises and flapped her wings in my face, but was eventually trussed up. The result looked not unlike a small child in a giant diaper.

Next, I strung this ensemble from a ceiling beam. Yvette could sit on the floor in her hen truss until I yanked on the string, causing the bird to rise and half support herself on her wobbly legs.

We'd start with five-minute sessions, and after a while she could stand up for half-hour stretches before keeling slightly sideways and looking more miserable than usual, or revolving slowly and self-consciously.

On other occasions I would haul her completely off the ground, grab her inert claws and cycle them round and round for a few minutes so that her joints and muscles didn't atrophy.

This process went on for weeks. I became inured to the stink of slightly fetid chicken and the odd odor of bird-shit-marinated broadsheet newspaper. Yvette also got used to me and, although I was clearly not her idea of fun, a certain coming to terms had taken place. She became pliant and resigned, a process helped by access to tinned sweetcorn, which she loved, and the occasional handful of raisins, which she really loved.

Most of our birds have been happy to eat out of our hands. Usually this doesn't hurt, but Yvette was both incredibly avaricious and clumsy, and would grab and twist beakfuls of my palm as she gobbled the raisins.

All chickens love food, but Yvette lacked the saving grace of cuteness. However, I looked at her lumpen profile and imagined the big, brown eggs she would eventually lay and pressed on.

It took about a month before I could ditch the truss and Yvette was able to stand unaided. Quite often she would need to be helped to her feet, but once there she would stand for hours at a stretch, looking bemused. Clearly, walking wasn't on her agenda, so I decided to use her favorite food as an incentive.

Taking the now statuesque Yvette into the garden I laid a trail of raisins for her and plonked the dim bird in front of it. She stared wistfully at them and stayed put. I went back into the shed to write 2,000 words on company car taxation, and came out half an hour later to find the raisins uneaten and Yvette sitting on the ground. I hauled her up again, picked up one of the tiny, dried fruits and proffered it just out of pecking reach.

With a sudden, goose-stepping lurch Yvette made for the food, tore it out of my hand and fell over. It was a start.

God knows whether our neighbors entertained themselves by watching the ludicrous pantomime that followed and went on for what seemed like a lifetime. It involved a man carrying a chicken into his back garden, making the chicken stand up, bending double and proffering something edible to the chicken, then walking backwards shouting encouragement as the bird half tap-danced, half goose-stepped after this prize.

BUTCH CHICK

It must have taken about three months from the time Yvette first fell over before she started to walk unaided. Her knee joints appeared to have partially seized up, causing her to move in a staccato, National Socialist way, but she was no longer sitting in her own filth and was able to get about quite easily. We felt a certain, slightly war-weary satisfaction as we watched this unattractive, greedy animal stamp around our garden, stopping to wrench plants out of the ground as she did so.

Soon we were able to move her in with our big hens, who fell upon her with the joy of seasoned playground bullies. Perhaps this had something to do with what happened next.

To start with, she continued in her role of hen-as-victim, but was still growing prodigiously and showed no signs of laying any eggs.

I was at work (in a proper office, for once) when the phone rang. It was my wife.

"Something's happened to Yvette," she said.

"Oh," I muttered, fearing the worst. Had the bird suffered a heart attack or used her new found mobility to escape?

"She's started crowing."

Yvette promptly proved the point by doing just that. Even over the phone I could tell this wasn't an Elvis-style half crow, but a full-blooded "Bosh! Give it some of that!" expostulation.

"I don't think it's a phase she's going through either," said Jane.

The vet found our next visit most amusing.

"Well," she said, peering up Yvette's rear with a special piece of kit of the sort a doctor might use to examine a child's ear. "You've got a bit of both here." Her shoulders were jiggling up and down as she tried to stop laughing.

"What exactly does that mean?" I asked.

"I can see both sets of sexual organs. Male and female. Not very well developed, but definitely there. As for what this means, well, this bird will probably always be a virgin—and don't expect any eggs."

So, after three months' nursing, six months' feeding, and at least $75 in vet's bills, we were the proud possessors of a camp, stiff-kneed, goose-stepping he/she chicken that was doomed to spend its life firing blanks. Fantastic.

Yvette was proof that chickens, like ducks, will sometimes change sex if you have an all-female flock, although I don't think they engage in the sort of gay gang-bangs beloved of drakes if there aren't enough female partners to go round. Hormonally, Elvis had gone slightly that way, but Yvette's more emphatic change of direction put an end to this, and Elvis gave up her semi-crowing activities.

The vet's diagnosis was right about the egg-laying bit, and I can't vouch for Yvette's capacity in the sperm department, as we never tried to raise any chicks from the eggs laid while s/he was around, but that bird definitely wasn't a virgin chicken.

MALE ASSERTIVENESS

Yvette—we tried rechristening the beast with a male name, but the fey one stuck—was a sex maniac of the Benny Hill-in-character variety, and was not a considerate lover. By now vastly bigger than Elvis, Mrs. Brown, and two more recent arrivals, Peckham and Egghead, Yvette's idea of foreplay consisted of doing a jerky war dance then flattening his unfortunate amour into the mud. It was rather like watching a tank run over a Mini, and would result in a great deal of pained squawking and flapping.

As Yvette's voraciousness increased, so his co-habitees' attempts to escape his inept attentions became more frantic. At the first sign of Yvette's clomping "Hello girls" dance, the "girls" would do their best to flee. Yvette soon discovered that the best route to a quick bunk-up was to sneak up on his prey and jump her from behind.

The organized bullying that had previously been a feature of our flock vanished. Everybody was, quite literally, too busy watching their backs. This was a positive feature of Yvette's presence. He was also the reason why one of our formerly more put-upon chickens had started to thrive.

EGGHEAD'S REPRIEVE

Egghead was, frankly, absurd-looking, with a worried little face that peeped from a cluster of feathers that resembled an Elizabethan ruff collar. She'd cost us $22 and was a rip-off, since

she had deformed feet, each with an extra set of gnarled toes, which Mrs. Brown and co. liked to peck until they bled.

The bullying grew so intense that this bird nearly starved to death, and I spent a week nursing her in a cardboard box in my office, proffering an endless supply of bread, currants, and the inevitable tinned sweetcorn.

She recovered and eventually teamed up again with Peckham, the hen we'd bought with her. A bird with a vulture's head stuck on a black and white chicken body, Peckham looked like a tough guy, but was thick and harmless. She also had a curious slave/parent relationship with Egghead, who was above Peckham in the pecking order but who insisted on retreating into chickhood and wheedling herself under Peckham at bedtime.

Given that they were both a similar size this made for some uncomfortable nights for Peckham as Egghead jammed herself head first under Peckham's front. These birds would sleep front to back, with Peckham standing up, legs splayed, to accommodate her companion, whose peevish countenance would peep out from beneath Peckham's fluffy posterior.

During the day they would walk round in file, taking almost identical steps and pecking at the ground at the same time; we wondered how one would survive without the other.

Nature plays cruel tricks, and it was the outwardly healthy Peckham who suddenly became ill and died, leaving her weaker partner to fend for herself. When Yvette decided boyhood was

the way to go, Egghead seized the moment and latched onto this stomping, selfish beast and became his number-one girlfriend, lolloping after him and putting up with his inept advances. It was clearly a survival mechanism and it appeared to work. Egghead grew chubby and healthy.

THE DAWN CHORUS

Our neighbors only once complained about the noise Yvette made in the early hours. We'd explained about acquiring an accidental rooster, and we told them that should his early morning outpourings wake them, they should tell us and we would re-house him.

The couple who lived immediately next door, and who had uncomplainingly put up with garden raids from Mrs. Brown, eventually had a quiet word.

Things had been fine until a few late summer nights when we'd forgotten to lock the birds in their hen-house, allowing them to get on with getting up at about 4 AM. Yvette celebrated these lapses with a series of full-volume vocal performances, which we didn't hear because we slept deeply with our bedroom window shut. The neighbors were light-sleeping fresh-air lovers, and the wife was enduring daily rail commutes to and from London.

Would we mind terribly, they asked, making sure we locked up the birds, as this at least contained the noise, and they could sleep through it.

Legally and morally they could have given us a hard time, and we realized we'd been lucky. The apparently innocent activity of keeping a few hens could have embroiled us in an unpleasant dispute. Although they didn't know it, by this stage we were already planning to move house to somewhere with a bigger garden where noise would be less of an issue.

YVETTE MEETS HIS MATCH

In the end Yvette didn't move with us. For a three-week period after we'd uprooted and I began the process of building the even more posh chicken run, he and the girls had stayed in temporary accommodation at the home of some chicken-keeping friends.

I was walking along High Street Kensington when my mobile phone rang. "I think you should come and see Elvis. She's gone bald."

Elvis wasn't completely featherless, but her appearance had changed totally. Her face was gray and her comb had flopped sideways and was the color of a tramp's gums. She was sadly lacking in neck feathers and her bottom and stomach were completely naked, as were her legs. All but one of her once luxuriant tail feathers had fallen out, too, and what remained of her plumage looked dull and unhealthy. She was also extremely skittish and nervous, thanks largely to Yvette's constant attempts to bonk her into the mud. In a more confined space she couldn't escape and had taken to hiding in the nest-box, which meant she wasn't getting to the food or water.

Given her advanced years (Elvis was at least five), we feared she would have a heart attack. Jane and I decided that one of them had to go. The idea of bidding Elvis farewell was unthinkable, but Yvette wasn't the most marketable of chickens, being of uncertain lineage and a stomping, witless thug.

Fortunately, the chicken-breeding lady from the castle farm said she could do with a big rooster to keep her lumbering Marin chickens happy. Yvette would fit the bill very well. I confess that we did not reveal the bird's past, and when Yvette's new owner said "What a funny walk it's got," we just nodded sagely but made no further comment.

Afterwards, as we drove away, there was no sense of regret. Under other, more pragmatic circumstances this worthless animal would have had his neck stretched, and we felt certain that the bird had once again landed on his enormous feet. He'd been put in a spacious enclosure with a substantial flock of jumbo-sized lady chickens who were much more his size and who could give him a wide berth if they wanted. The only problem we could see was that this space was shared with a flock of ducks and drakes. Given Yvette's lack of discrimination, we wondered if they were about to be in for a nasty surprise.

The Boys

GERALD

After our experience with Yvette, we decided that it would be a good idea to find a replacement that had his good points but did not suffer from any of his vices.

Our two bantams, Satan and BB, had carried on living in separate accommodation. A previous pre-Yvette attempt at putting them in with the big girls had resulted in ill feeling and violence. One morning I noticed that the smallest bird, BB, seemed to have a slightly injured wing. As I watched her scratching about on the ground, Elvis came out of the raised hen-house and stood on the old kitchen stool the birds used as a perch. She took careful aim and then jumped onto the tiny bird, keeping her wings folded for maximum squashing effect. After that it was back to separate runs and mutual recrimination.

Things didn't improve after Yvette did her sexual volte-face, because he clearly wanted to have his inept way with BB, who was the size of a fat pigeon. The result would have been too eye-watering to contemplate, and that meant a rapprochement still wasn't possible.

This was why we decided to get a bantam rooster. He could still try his love-god routine with the full-sized hens—although proving it might be physically difficult—and be a suitable other half for Satan and BB, who could finally be introduced with the big hens, in what would then, we hoped, be a virtually bully-free zone.

So we had high hopes as we collected Gerald, a bantam cross-breed with the slightly pompous air of a Victorian industrialist. He had a careful, waddling walk and wings that gave him a hands-clasped-behind-the-back stance that would have suited a stove pipe hat and a big cigar. Inevitably he came from the castle farm, and was effectively a trade-in for Yvette.

He also had a waistcoat-like swathe of brightly colored feathers and was rather attractive in a neckless, circular way. We thought we were on to a winner, although his previous owner said that if things didn't work out she'd exchange him for another bird.

Gerald was introduced to the full-sized hens, and after a little deliberation walked rotundly into the chicken house and for the next couple of days barely put in an appearance.

We began to feel a little concerned and opened the door a crack to see our new rooster cowering in the far corner as Mrs. Brown made her way over to him and pecked the top of his head.

We removed Gerald from this humiliating hell-hole and put him in the old cat box used as emergency chicken accommodation. His extreme keenness to eat and drink indicated that he hadn't seen much in the way of food and water.

"Oh," said the castle farm lady when we explained our predicament. "He probably isn't fully mature and hasn't been able to handle your birds. That happens sometimes." Basically, having lived with a bastard chicken our old broilers had decided that Gerald wasn't man enough for them.

ZORRO

Which is how Zorro came into our lives. A kind of jungle fowl, he was a full-sized bird but not huge. With his showy red comb and wattles, giant cream ear lobes, an explosion of tail feathers, and shimmering plumage of golds, greens, and blacks, he had a dashing handsomeness that marked him out as an instant male tart.

Chickens apparently see in color, so this raffishness was not going to be lost on our girls.

When we first introduced him to the flock Zorro wasn't fully mature either, and Mrs. Brown was initially unconvinced of

his physical charms. He strode into the run and started to scratch about, and Elvis and Egghead stared nervously at this exotic apparition. Mrs. B, who is good at adopting a threatening posture, went up to him and gave Zorro a look that said, "I'm staring very hard at you—what are you going to do about it?"

Zorro continued to forage, so Mrs. B stuffed her face close to his and glared. Zorro stopped, looked mildly at Mrs. Brown and carried on as before. This was not the effect she was looking for, so she stuck her beak as close as she could to Zorro's head and when that didn't elicit a suitably cowering response she pecked him.

Zorro puffed up his chest feathers and charged Mrs. Brown who went "Aaaagh!" and ran to the far corner of the run where she, Elvis, and Egghead gibbered and clucked. Zorro went back to eating and nobody tried it on with him again.

As he matured he proved to be rather charming, letting his wives eat first and clucking loudly and excitedly if he found something he thought they would particularly enjoy.

He learned to crow and developed an unsurprising interest in sex, but not weighing the chicken equivalent of 250 pounds or possessing the seduction technique of a ball-and-chain meant that his partners were left feeling ruffled but not punch-drunk. He was quite friendly with us to begin with, even eating out of our hands, until the morning I was forced to give Mrs. Brown a short course of antibiotics, which she resisted in the usual way.

I was on my haunches clasping the unhappy patient when I became aware that something vaguely sharp was colliding with my backside. Zorro, convinced that I was attacking Mrs. Brown, was running up and down, pecking and drop-kicking my bottom. It wasn't very painful, and in a way I was pleased. I hoped that this instinctive response would protect them against our daft dog, Hoover, who, when bored, enjoyed frightening the chickens. Being a terrier crossbreed, we didn't doubt that he would kill our birds if he ever got among them, on the basis that it would be fun to play with them until they broke.

Zorro would have been quickly dispatched by Hoover too, but separated by the chicken wire, dog and bird harmlessly squared up to each other, and when Hoover charged, Zorro charged back, bringing the dog up short. Quite often Hoover would back off, although to avoid reinforcing bad canine behavior this was something we discouraged.

Some roosters can be vicious, chasing and attacking their owners, and they're capable of causing real injury. As Zorro grew bolder he began charging us, too. This became a ritual when we came to feed or clean out the birds. He also took to pecking my Wellington boots, and if I attempted to hand-feed the flock he would more or less jump up and down on my hand, furiously scattering pellets as he did so.

We were happy that he was protecting his wives, but concerned that he was starting to control us as well as them. If

we'd been parents of small children his antics would have been more worrying still. He was capable of hurting—and certainly frightening—a small child.

TOUGH LOVE

"It says we have to cuddle him," said Jane, looking up from one of our "How to. . ." chicken-keeping books. "If he goes for you, pick him up and hold him and talk to him until he stops struggling. Apparently we should have done this before he started to mature, but it's worth a try."

Wearing a solid pair of gloves and some clear plastic goggles kept for when I'm forced to trim the flower-beds, I went in search of macho confrontation. Initially Zorro was happy to oblige. Neck feathers puffed out, he danced round my Wellingtons like a boxer looking for a killer punch, and was clearly less than pleased when I went on the attack. When I caught him, he wriggled furiously before giving up. He didn't try to peck me, but instead looked up at me with sullen resignation.

As I tickled him under the chin, round the back of his jawbone and between his shoulder blades (bliss for tamer birds) you could almost see the inner struggle going on in his small, testosterone-crazed head, along the lines of, "You bastard! I hate you! I really hate you! Oooo, this is quite nice. Bastard! Bastard! Yes, that's better. Touch my birds and you're dead! Keeping going under the wings, particularly the left one. Bastard!"

I eventually released my grip and kept tickling, and it took him some 30 seconds to realize that he could escape. Zorro leapt from my lap and made for the farthest corner of the run.

Another rooster-calming technique, which we haven't tried, is to mimic the wing-tip-waggling sideways dance aggressive roosters make, together with the noises, so that both bird and human engage in a sort of line-dance stand-off. This ends with the human gently but firmly shunting the bird up the backside with his or her boot, knocking him off balance.

This sounds fine in theory, but anyone watching a grown man in a chicken run clucking, making wing-flapping gestures, and dancing from side to side might get the wrong impression.

Zorro still tries it on occasionally, but when this happens he suffers the indignity of "tough love" and stares at me with impotent, malevolent loathing as we go though the tickling ritual. Jane and I reckon it's time well spent, since a behavior that was starting to grow increasingly nasty seems to have been checked.

As for Zorro's inevitable crowing activities, the noise mostly seems to come in bursts and is usually started when a neighboring rooster announces his presence. He and Zorro engage in a series of "If you think you're so tough come here and say that" exchanges. The fact that this bird lives at the other end of the village doesn't seem to matter, and that the two have never clapped eyes on each other and never will is also irrelevant. For Zorro and his unseen enemy it's the thought that counts.

The Birds

OUR FLOCK AS IT IS NOW

As I write, our current flock consists of Zorro, Egghead, Tikka, Delia, Hendon, Baggy Chicken, Elvis, and Mrs. Brown.

After Satan keeled over, Bald Bird was left in less-than-splendid isolation due, it must be said, to behavioral problems. She liked people but could not stand other chickens. Zorro was tolerable because he was a bloke, and to start with I shared him between her and the big girls, but attempts at moving everybody in together were thwarted by BB constantly trying to beat up birds that were three times her size.

I put a small wire run inside the big chicken enclosure, decanted BB into this and hoped that close proximity would breed familiarity. It's a method that usually works after a few days, but not with BB. Instead, this bird spent a lot of time shrieking and trying to peck her neighbors through the mesh.

Eventually an uneasy calm descended and I made the mistake of letting BB out. She charged Egghead and instantly vanished under a scrum of angry chickens. Zorro tried to break up the mêlée, but everyone was too furious to notice. I pulled the by-now dishevelled BB from this thrashing mass and admitted defeat.

On her own, BB looked slightly depressed, but we didn't want to get another bantam companion because of her age (it could well leave us with a similar chicken-on-her-own problem

when BB dropped off her perch), and anyway it seemed unlikely that she would welcome the company. So I phoned Madge Cooper.

Madge, a former neighbor, had become smitten with our birds, had looked after them when we'd moved house, and now owned some bantams of her own. Perhaps BB would cope better if she moved in with hens her own size who already had an established pecking order that she'd have to enter at the bottom.

"Yes of course I'll take her," said Madge.

We said goodbye to the irritable BB with mixed feelings, and left it for a few weeks before phoning and asking for a progress report.

"Well," said Madge. "She's lovely with the grandchildren. Really friendly. They can pick her up and stroke her. She really likes that. What did you say she was called?"

"Bald Bird."

"They call her 'Baby,'" said Madge.

Oh well, I thought, then asked "How's she getting on with the other hens?"

There was a pause. "She's still on her own. We put her in with the others and it worked for a bit, but she's very aggressive."

So that was that. We'd raised an irredeemably hen-hating chicken. Despite being offered a fresh start in a run with three roosters and birds her own size, BB, or "Baby," could not get along with her own kind and demonstrated this by going on the attack. It was back, permanently, to the isolation hutch where, between bouts of being loved enthusiastically by small children, BB found other means of entertainment.

"I visited Madge and saw that chicken you gave to her," said Sue, who works in the village shop. "It doesn't like the others, does it? It goes——" (she blew a long raspberry and made a series of rapid V-sign gestures). I knew just what she meant.

Nevertheless, BB's departure resulted in our having a flock of full-sized birds for the first time and also had the advantage that they were all living in one place.

DO IT YOURSELF DO'S

At our current home I set about my second attempt at chicken-run building and the end result was rather better put together than the first. It involved a cheap, self-assembly garden shed. In its sides I chopped two hen-sized holes and made two hinged trapdoors to cover these, then spent several sweaty weekends building aviaries on either side of the shed. I sank the chicken wire into the ground and put paving slabs round the outside as a fox deterrent.

These enclosures could be used in rotation, allowing the ground to recover and hopefully reducing the risk of nasty earthborn diseases.

I made a separate nest-box at the back, so that we didn't have to squelch across the roosting area's pooped-on floor, and fitted a long perch with a second smaller, lower perch for the hens to hop on to when negotiating the bigger roosting area. If hens have to jump down from a perch that's too high they can injure their feet.

111

The new housing was more spacious and much easier to clean than the first hen-house, although it took the birds several weeks to work out what the perch was for. I'd help by putting them on it. They would complain and get off it again, but eventually they got the message.

EXPANSION

The extra space allowed us to increase the size of our flock, but the birds we purchased to do this were bought on the rebound. We live near the Rare Breeds Center in Woodchurch, Kent, an animal sanctuary that specializes in propagating rare farm animals, including chickens. It's partially staffed by adults with special needs, whose skill and knowledge is a complement to them and the work done at the center. The place is a great font of avian knowledge and well worth a visit. It was also to be the venue for a chicken auction. We reckoned this would be the perfect opportunity to find some distinctive, unusual birds.

The auction was held in a small marquee, with cages propped up on bales of hay. Each cage contained hens that were exotic in varying degrees. We made our selections and were soundly outbid every time.

Suffering from hen-purchase withdrawal symptoms we went home, flipped through a local free-ads paper and discovered somebody selling ex-free-range farm hens for $1.50 each. Naturally we phoned them at once, then set off to visit.

"Don't touch the electric fence," said the vendor, a fierce-looking middle-aged lady. "It's wired into the mains. I can't keep the bloody foxes out otherwise."

Shuddering slightly at the thought of sizzling vixen we made our way into a sort of giant hen prison camp. It wasn't a cruel environment, but it wasn't very cheerful either. Generations of chickens had compacted the ground into a hard mud crust. There were high fences and thoroughly lived-in sheds. Hundreds of identical brown farmyard hens milled about, pecked, and looked vacant.

There were a few roosters to enliven things somewhat, and one brilliant white chicken.

"That one's not for sale. She's my pet," said the vendor.

Confronted with a sea of otherwise outwardly similar birds we dithered. Should we have the one with the slightly better plumage or the one that looked a bit sad? As usual, I had my eye on a particularly battered and featherless creature, but Jane gave me a "Be sensible" look. I hardened my heart and we moved on.

"They're all in lay," said the electric-fence matron, who was clearly finding our indecision a bit of a trial and started catching birds and showing them to us in an attempt to speed things up.

We'd decided on buying three hens and had selected two when I found two more candidates.

"I try and sell as many of them as I can to people like you," said the woman. "In the past they've gone to a local zoo. They get fed to the lions, but it always seems a bit drastic to me."

We looked at our quartet, and both had the same thought: "We really ought to put one back."

"Tell you what," said the woman, who clearly wanted us to go away, "Take four for the price of three."

There was a subtext here. Have a free chicken or it becomes lion food. This was an offer we couldn't refuse.

A MOTLEY CREW

So, having started the day looking for three young, semi-exotic birds we ended up with four utterly ordinary broilers, one of which had a droopy eye that made her look a bit like Robert Mitchum with a beak. This was the bird we came to know as Baggy Chicken.

We'd learned enough about hen socialization not to stick them straight into the run with our existing birds. We have a small, separate wire enclosure for housing ill or broody hens, so we put it alongside the big run and unloaded our latest foursome into this. Their arrival created intense interest among our existing flock. There was much mutual reptilian peering (chickens have the birdie trait of being descended from reptiles—the scales on their legs are a relic of this) and slightly guttural "Who are you then?" noises. We left them to get acquainted until dusk, when Mrs. Brown and co. had trundled off to roost, then put the new birds in with them.

Over the next few days there was some low-intensity bullying, but nothing like the Bossy Chicken-era feather wrenching. This was partly due to Zorro protecting the latest additions to his harem and partly because everyone had been given the chance of sizing each other up first.

It took about a week for an expanded pecking order to be established, and the most consistent bully turned out to be Egghead, who had previously been at the bottom of the social

pile. Now, finding herself slap bang in the middle, she was determined to exercise her newly acquired power, although generally this was limited to a series of half-hearted lunges at meal times.

After Zorro, the ancient but still slightly demented Elvis is notionally the bird in charge, although she expends more energy on being terrified by the lawnmower than roughing up her cohorts. She's certainly higher up the social ladder than the stout Mrs. Brown, who nevertheless has control-freak tendencies when given the chance. Then there's Egghead, who occasionally has the demeanor of a once-bullied schoolchild who, despite having been made class president, will always lack natural authority.

As for our newest arrivals, known collectively as "the Stringy Quartet," some sort of pecking order exists, but who's in charge of whom isn't clear to me, which happily indicates a general lack of bullying among them.

We don't have a friction-free flock, but the regular bouts of assault and battery are, for the moment, a thing of the past.

11

Eggs
and a Potted History

AN OLD JOKE

A hen and an egg are sitting up in bed together. The hen lights up a post-coital cigarette and takes a long, satisfied drag. "Well," says the egg, "that answers the question about who came first."

Yes, this is a terrible joke, but since this is a chapter intended more or less to answer the question it poses I'm delighted to use the opportunity for some gratuitous smut. The honest answer to the age-old question of "Which came first? . . ." is that reptiles came before birds, and birds are their warm-blooded cousins. The scales on a chicken's legs are an evolutionary nod to its connection to such uncuddly creatures as the pterodactyl. Feathers, too, are latter-day substitutes for scales.

Egg-laying is another common bond. You might think of an egg as basically being made from three components: shell, white, and yolk; however, when that egg is fertile and an embryo starts to develop, it could almost be regarded as a single entity. When a super-heated, broody chicken plants herself on a clutch of eggs and starts the slow-cooking process towards birth, it takes about four days for things to really begin happening.

CANDLING

You can see what's going on within the egg by using the quaintly named process called "candling." This involves holding an egg in front of a lit candle to assess its contents for freshness and blood spots. Some people aren't keen to find these things in their

breakfast eggs, and candling was tied up with the practice of stamping a red British Lion insignia on eggs that met the blood-free standards set by the Ministry of Scrambling, or whatever.

I'm not clear whether this practice was tied in with the "Go To Work On An Egg" advertising campaign of the 1960s, thought up, according to some sources, by the novelist Salman Rushdie, or "Salmonella Rushdie" as we must now call him.

You can actually buy an electric candling lamp, which looks a bit like a hairdryer. The egg is placed against the business end of this and the lamp is lit. It's also possible to make your own candler by sticking a light source into a box with a small hole—about 3 centimeters in diameter—made in one end of it.

Either way, eggs can be checked after being incubated for seven and then 14 days, although it's important to keep them the same way up and hold them sideways so that their contents aren't battered about.

After a week, if the egg is active you'll see a pea-sized embryo with blood vessels radiating from it. You should also be able to make out the beginnings of an air sac at the egg's chubbier end. This will be paler than the rest of its contents. Apparently, if you see an ill-defined, swirling dark mass this indicates that the egg is addled and has therefore had it.

A week later and it should be possible to see that the embryo has now grown to about the size of a quarter, and will have easily defined blood vessels. Candling is only worth doing if you want

119

to remove dud eggs before hatching, but it's not something we've ever tried, partly because we like to be surprised and because not disturbing the hormone-crazed broody hen strikes us as both pragmatic and kind.

LIFE INSIDE THE EGG

To allow the rapidly developing embryo to breathe in its apparently hermetically sealed home, it is connected by a vein and a couple of arteries to a collection of blood vessels inside the lining of the egg shell. It is these items that keep the chick supplied with oxygen. Even as the chick starts to break out of the shell this system keeps working, and the lungs take over only once it has struggled into the outside world for the first time. At this stage not only does the baby hen have two methods of breathing, but it also effectively has two digestive systems, one that has kept it alive during the incubation period and the other being developed for when it first lusts after worms and leftover vegetables.

During its fetal development yet more veins join the embryo to the yolk and egg white (aka the albumen), linking the bird fetus to the contents of the egg and getting nourishment from them. These veins have "septa" membranes that extend along the yolk in folds, effectively digesting it and transferring the nutrients into the embryo's bloodstream. So at this stage it's less "Which came first, chicken or egg?" and more "Which is which?"

Even before hatching takes place the chick starts using its lungs to breathe and the air sac at the "blunt" end of the egg. This is where the animal pokes its head en route to breaking out of its shell. On hatching the putative hen leaves the remains of the egg behind, but the last of the energy taken from the yolk is absorbed and used by the chick to keep going during the first hours of its new life. It can be up to 48 hours before the tiny, vulnerable animal needs to feed for the first time.

Eggs have to be veritable storehouses of nutrients. Although the white is 90 percent water, it also contains proteins, while half the yolk is made up of fats and proteins. Overall, the guts of an egg contains 14 percent protein and 10 percent fat. It's also stuffed with various vitamins.

When fertile and incubated, an egg needs all these elements to sustain a fast-growing occupant for three weeks, and this helps explain why, when minus chick and/or unfertilized, it's a very good food source for people, but a bit risky when eaten to excess for those with high cholesterol levels.

HEN'S TEETH

You might be surprised to know that very young chickens have teeth, or at least a single tooth. This is basically an excrescence attached to the end of a chick's upper mandible—that's the top half of its beak. This is known in the trade as the "egg tooth" or "shell-cutter." Having made it into the air sac, the baby hen uses

this to press against the inside of the eggshell until this starts to crack outwards. This has the rather charming name of "pipping."

By this stage instinct is hard at work. The chick starts to revolve inside the egg, using the "tooth" to enlarge the crack as it does so. Then it pushes with its feet to exert pressure on the damaged shell with its skull. Soon a small, bleary head emerges, often topped off with the cap of the shell, and after some

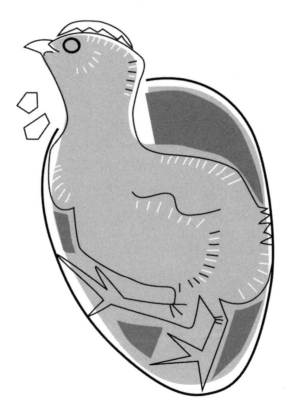

struggling and wriggling the chick emerges from what was effectively its birth capsule. To call an egg a biosphere might sound a bit pretentious, but that's really what it is. As for the chick's egg tooth, this drops off after a couple of days.

EGG-TURNING

For the bird's previous, egg-bound three weeks, its mother will have been turning the eggs several times a day so that their embryos don't stay in one place. The embryo can stick to the inner shell membranes and the movement keeps the chick away from any buildup of embryo detritus and assists the vitelline breathing system. Anybody rearing chicks using an incubator will be familiar with egg-turning and marking the eggs with a felt-tip cross so that they know which way up they should go. If this isn't done regularly, birds can be born with a range of problems, including deformities.

There's really no excuse for poor egg management since people have been rearing hens by artificial means since well before the birth of Christ. Incubators were around in China back in about 1400 B.C. Ancient Egyptians reared chickens, too, complete with live-in helpers whose job was to turn the eggs, generally look after their occupants, and, presumably, sweat copiously and unpleasantly in the hot conditions.

As a career choice this does not greatly appeal to me. However, spending three weeks with a bunch of eggs in a hot,

fly-infested incubator is surely still preferable to being either a spouse or servant of a Pharaoh who drops dead before you do, as being a member of his entourage you stood a very good chance of being bumped off and entombed with him so that you would be ready and waiting in the next world to help him en route to divinity. Turning eggs, feeding chicks, and shovelling shit suddenly become far more attractive.

Whether Akhenaten, Seti, Rameses, et al liked their eggs boiled, fried, or even "on the side" is hardly a major historical issue. However, the fact that domestic chickens were trundling around Ancient Egypt indicates that the antecedents of Mrs. Brown, Elvis, and co. have been scratching about next to human beings for a very long time.

THE FAMILY TREE

Today, most people who know about such things reckon that the domestic chicken—aka *Gallus domesticus*—is now the planet's most numerous bird species, with around nine billion of the little buggers born every year.

Elvis and co. are descended from *Gallus gallus*, or jungle fowl, forest-dwelling birds still found in the Indian subcontinent and of which there were four distinct strains. One, the Red jungle fowl, is reckoned to have been domesticated first. This could have happened in 3000–4000 B.C. (the odd thousand years being small change in evolutionary terms), so this bird is

most directly the daddy—and indeed the mummy—of today's ill-tempered bantams and fat-buttocked farmyard hens.

All this means that chickens are not only the world's most populous birds but were also its first domesticated ones.

COMMON TRAITS

Anybody encountering wild jungle fowl would find them pretty familiar. They spend their waking hours in flocks, trundling about the forest floor in search of worms, creepy-crawlies, and plant seeds, using a rapid pecking action to gobble them up.

Each flock is overseen by a relentlessly misogynistic dominant male who lives a lad's magazine-reader's wet dream of shagging, fighting, and generally being keen on eugenics with spurs and feathers, as long as his genes triumph.

The average Asian jungle has rather more predators than an English farmyard, yet like regular modern chickens undomesticated jungle fowl aren't very good at flying; instead they are well versed in that flapping/running thing hens do to work up a good speed and get away from you.

Perching and roosting are other things they both have in common, and if you pick up even the dimmest domestic bird and gently move its body up and down, the animal's head will stay absolutely steady. This is a legacy of having to stand on windblown tree branches and see what's going on around you.

125

Preening and enjoying dust-bathing are common traits of domestic and wild birds, and both have preen glands sited near their rear ends. These glands secrete oil, which birds take with their beaks to give their feathers that Brylcreamed look

demanded by all right-thinking chickens. Taking dust baths—a very common avian pleasure—is a lovely way to mangle body parasites and be sociable, whether you live in a Javanese jungle or by a muddy field in England.

EATING AND BREEDING

Given that they eat anything that moves or sprouts, jungle fowl and their ilk have suitably case-hardened digestive systems. Recently consumed grubs, seeds, et al are stored in the crop, a sac located under the neck. Digestion takes place partly in the gut and partly in the gizzard. If you've always yearned to know what the gizzard does but never dared ask, read on.

The gizzard is basically a crushing machine in the form of a sac filled with any grit taken down with the food. It's surrounded by powerful muscles, which, with the grit, crush any food contents. A lack of grit can lead to stomach upsets or worse. Again, all this is eminently familiar to anyone who has kept chickens.

The wild and the domesticated birds also share breeding habits. After laying about six eggs in a dark, secluded spot (likely to have been hollowed out for the purpose), the jungle fowl mother-to-be will spend the next three weeks incubating them.

The chicks are almost instantly mobile, and don't need external feeding for the first day or two of life. Again, this is *vin ordinaire* to domestic hens and gives both them and their wild

counterparts a fighting chance of avoiding dangers in a predator-laden environment.

As to why birds in general—and hens in particular—lay eggs at all, I found a good answer in an entertainingly written book called *The Backyard Poultry Book* by Andrew Singer. Dating from 1976, it's probably long out of print (our copy came from a rummage sale). It suggests that not having to cart babies around inside you aids speed and lightness. Useful for keeping ahead of creatures that want to eat you and less tiring when you have to go foraging.

CHICKEN-KEEPING THROUGH THE AGES

It reveals something about the human mind that when first domesticated, chickens were bred for cock-fighting rather than as a food resource.

In the ancient world there was even a five-level chicken caste system, with the most violent strain, the *asil*, being reserved for royalty, and lesser species rigidly allocated to those lower down this depressingly enduring human pecking order.

As domestic fowl spread, new subspecies started to merge. The Javanese bred ornamental birds, for example, and the word "bantam" is thought to be a corruption of *ban tom*, a Javanese term meaning "small fowl."

As various pockets of humanity built empires, conquered one another, and retreated, so chickens came with them,

spreading across the planet as they did so. By 700 B.C., Persian soldiers who had conquered India had brought home chickens as one of the less obvious spoils of war.

By 500 B.C., Alexander the Great was bringing the birds into Europe, and cock-fighting remained a driving force behind the chicken's dash for world domination. Indeed, the Greeks enjoyed the bloody spectacle so much that roosters tearing each other to bits was an Olympic sport.

The Romans did their bit, too. By the time Julius Caesar arrived in Britain—about 55 B.C.—cock-fighting was part of English life, and students of ancient history will be able to tell you that some Roman legions used rooster motifs to show just how tough they were.

When Christopher Columbus arrived in America he brought chickens with him, and the Indians who weren't wiped out by succeeding generations of invaders took to chicken-keeping with enthusiasm, developing new breeds and strains to suit local conditions. This has been a feature of chicken-breeding from the beginning.

By the 1800s there was an explosion of interest in refining and creating new strains of hen. As the Victorian era got underway and Charles Darwin's theories became widely known, so it became fashionable to create improved (or at least different) animals. Many of today's most familiar chicken breeds first showed their wattled faces at this time. Orpingtons are an example of this.

By 1865, the Poultry Club of Great Britain (which is still very much with us) developed its "standards of excellence" for the first time. There became a sort of official guide to what was in, and what was out, in the world of chickens.

THE MODERN CHICKEN

British and Italian hen-obsessives were the prime movers in evolving the standard breeds to become the chunky egg-machines we know today, with their American counterparts closely involved after about 1850. By the 1970s, the UK national average for annual egg-laying was 228 eggs. One bird managed 361 eggs, and must have felt very baggy and exhausted afterwards. This compares with an average of 30 eggs a year produced by a wild jungle fowl, which is also likely to become broody three times a year. Broodiness is important if you live in a dangerous place and need to breed regularly, but danger is also something that would rather take your tiny mind off laying eggs.

One big difference between wild and domestic birds is that the former lay only fertile eggs. Why waste energy producing something that has no value? In the jungle, eggs exist to further the species, not to fill freezers in the local supermarket. The effective industrialization of chicken-farming really started to happen during the first World War, when sustaining and increasing food production became vital; this was further evolved during the second World War, for obvious reasons.

Birds that became known as "hybrids" (standard, wide-hipped, and, in this country, usually brown-feathered hens) were developed in America between the wars. Without going into massive detail about chicken eugenics, hybrid hens are the product of mating certain pure-breed birds (such as Rhode Island Reds and Leghorns) to get the best qualities of both—viz temperament, the number of eggs laid, the amount of meat they produce, etc. Some of the resultant offspring will improve on the qualities of their mixed parentage, others will regress. Ruthlessly eliminate the latter breed from the former and super-chickens with strange ideas of flying to Brazil and producing identical versions of themselves result. Soon the world's hen-houses will be infiltrated by glassy-eyed zealot chickens, all clucking in a sinister way and telling a cowed and terrified animal kingdom, "We have ways of making you squawk!"

OK, that hasn't actually happened, but for *Gallus domesticus* the route from the jungle to the farm has been the result of deliberate man-made breeding programs. Given that man is part of the natural cycle, this is either a continuation of evolution or, if you regard this sort of thing as interfering with nature, a form of cloning. Since our newspapers seem to be filled with stories about the potential for cloned human beings, it's perhaps worth bearing in mind that we've been mucking around with the genetic make-up of other species for hundreds of years. Is this a good thing? Perhaps this is something to discuss over a chicken dinner.

The mindset that allowed this to happen can really be traced back to those bewhiskered, top-hatted Victorians for whom nature seemed to be an uncivilized irritant that needed teaching some manners. Since the Victorians are all dead it seems that nature won in the end, and many of the older breeds of chicken that had their DNA shunted together en route to making the modern hybrid are still doing their thing in a field or a barn near you.

CHAPTER

Mrs. Brown

Theatrical antics

Chickens themselves couldn't care less about matters of life and death. Our flock's meager brains are taken up with eating, sleeping, bullying, shagging, or being shagged.

Bossy Chicken is, sadly, no longer around to ponder these fundamentals of chicken life. She succumbed to "vent gleet," a disease involving nasty discharges from the nether regions. This bug also got Edith, the bird mentioned at the very start of this book—it was the reason for her being delicately attached to a vet's index finger.

Edith's eventual demise was the reason Mrs. Brown came into our lives, and, in a way, her story encapsulates why we keep chickens, and the pleasures and frustrations involved. I had planted Edith's still-warm mortal remains in the back garden, looked at our denuded hen-house, and decided to act unilaterally and buy another ordinary, brown chicken. A commercial breeder was situated about five miles away and would sell me a young "point of lay" bird (that is, an adolescent hen on the verge of her egg-laying career) for $5.

There was a snag. I also had to go to London to see a family friend who had recently been widowed and needed some company. The logical and probably kinder thing to do would have been to leave chicken-buying until later. Instead, I found a cardboard box, purchased a chicken, and set off on the 70-mile journey to town.

The bird was very quiet, but through a gap in the top of the box I could see a round eye regarding me in a way that indicated its owner wished she was somewhere else. The person I was visiting is an actress. Her husband had been a successful character actor and theater impresario, and she was involved in the emotionally draining task of arranging his memorial service.

She was on the telephone when I arrived carrying the cardboard box. I was ushered into her living room and she went back to the phone call, which had a grim circularity to it.

What I did next would have been in very bad taste for many people, but both she and her husband had shared a strong sense of the ridiculous. I'd known them since I was a toddler and reckoned a small, middle-finger gesture at fate would not go amiss. So I opened the box.

"Yes, it's bloody awful and. . .Oh my God there's a chicken. No, no, not a cooked one. I mean a real one. Yes, a live one. In my sitting-room."

The bird in the box had stood up and was looking at the inside of a living-room in Kew in southwest London with some surprise. She made no attempt to get out of the box and, as we all regarded each other, at least two of us enjoyed the incongruousness of the situation.

If this doesn't smack of gratuitous name-dropping, the person on the other end of the phone was the actor Sir Alan Bates, who treated this hen-happening as if it was quite unremarkable.

You might think this was a selfish thing to do to a farm animal. Perhaps it was, and although the bird was remarkably silent and watchful she did not seem stressed. She showed interest in the pieces of bread offered to her and was happy to

drink some water from a saucer that was usually the exclusive preserve of the household cat. Her presence also seemed to puncture a slightly despairing atmosphere, and this made the trip worthwhile.

HEPHZIBAH

It was heading for midnight when I got home and popped our new purchase into the nest-box with her bedfellows. My wife was fast asleep and I decided that waking her up to explain why I'd brought another animal into our lives without discussing this with her first might not go down too well.

When Jane spotted our new arrival the following morning she was not impressed.

Why hadn't I talked to her about it first? Weren't they our birds? Didn't she have a right to be consulted about further chicken acquisition?

I made some non-committal mumbling noises.

"What's it called?" she asked, when maintaining an air of disapproval finally became too much of an effort.

"Hephzibah, I think."

During the last war my actress friend had been a child in Ilford, where her mother had bought some chickens as a patriotic means of being more self-sufficient, something many city families did at the time. Rabbits were popular for the same reason, and although many birds and bunnies ended up feeding hard-pressed

wartime families, a number actually shared precious food rations without themselves ever quite ending up on the menu.

One of the Ilford birds liked laying its eggs behind a big-band era radio, presumably because it was warm. Another had an obsession with sewing machines and would jiggle its head in time with the movement of the needle when the mother was mending or making clothes. The faster the needle moved, the more its head waggled up and down.

The hens used to roost in a tree at the bottom of the garden, and one night some passing Luftwaffe pilots went in for some culling when they strafed the streets with machine-gun fire.

One of these animals had been called Hephzibah, and this is what our new arrival was christened by my friend. This remains her official first name, but inevitably an appropriate moniker found her rather than the other way round. The bird had a demeanor that vaguely reminded us of Queen Victoria, and she was brown. The film *Mrs. Brown* had recently been on television and that, basically, was that.

MRS. B MAKES FRIENDS

Mrs. Brown proved to be an immensely tame, nosey bird, who seemed to enjoy the company of people. Initially she wasn't keen on her fellow hens, who went through the usual ritual of giving her a hard time. During this early period she particularly endeared herself to me on one of my visits to the chicken-run.

I'd climbed in and was sitting on an upturned tree branch we'd put in there as a perch, and she jumped up on my lap, a gesture that had more to do with being left alone by the others than being pleased to see me.

Soon we were releasing Mrs. B into the garden, much to the annoyance of the rest of the flock who complained loudly as she followed us around. If we were weeding or digging, Mrs. Brown would look intently at what we were doing and attempt to join in. Freshly dug holes held a particular fascination for her since they often contained worms. This made digging a potentially hazardous activity for her as she developed a knack of jumping into the hole just as you were plunging the spade towards it.

One day we found a scruffy-looking golf ball in a flower-bed, threw it up the garden, and were surprised to see Mrs. Brown chasing it enthusiastically. We did this again and Mrs. B hurled herself after it once more. This became a comic ritual until she eventually worked out that golf balls weren't edible.

She also became determinedly territorial. We had a bird-table that she began to stalk. Any tit, pigeon, or rook foolish enough to try pecking the ground near it was soon being ambushed by a lumbering, wing-flapping brown chicken who would erupt from under a bush and charge them.

Presumably because we offered food and protection she treated us with a lot more tolerance. One summer's afternoon,

after a long relaxing lunch, I decided to take a snooze in the garden, flopped on the lawn, and went to sleep. After some time I became aware of a sort of cooing noise, opened an eye and saw Mrs. B sitting about a foot away from my head. Having finished preening her vent feathers (a lovely vista at eye level) she too nodded off.

Democracy eventually dictated that if Mrs. Brown was allowed out then so were the others, but initially they didn't share her wish to fraternize in quite the same way, which meant it was Mrs. B who first made the attempt to move into the house with us.

Our earliest inkling of her cunning plan came when we found a large Mr. Softee ice cream-shaped chicken turd on the dining-room floor. Some determined clucking from under the table also gave the game away.

Having expelled our unwanted guest (cue much running round furniture followed by indignant flapping and squawking), Jane handed me the pet-stain remover and a roll of kitchen towel.

"You can clear that up," she said brightly.

During the summer we liked leaving the back door open, and a brief war of attrition between home owners and hen followed. We thought victory was ours after purchasing one of those long bead curtains for doors as this had Mrs. Brown flummoxed for several months.

We'd see her peering at the curtain and chortled inwardly as we imagined a big, cartoon question mark appearing over her

head. Then she would toddle back up the garden. We knew our defenses had been breached when Jane was interrupted from a long phone call by a clucked greeting and saw a familiar feathered visage standing in the middle of the living-room.

After Mrs. Brown made it halfway up the stairs we gave up and kept the back door closed when she was on the loose.

She did get lost on a couple of nights when we left her out for too long and it grew dark. We had to borrow a storm lamp and crawl around in the undergrowth looking for her, but she had roosted quietly and successfully. On both occasions we were lucky. At dawn she emerged in next-door's garden, jumped onto one of their dustbins, and made enough noise to wake them and us up.

"It's alright, we don't mind Mrs. Brown," they said stoically. Apparently they still didn't mind Mrs. Brown when she took to perching on the bottom half of the split-level door that led from their garden into their kitchen.

When she started to produce eggs they were mind-bogglingly huge. She was laying five or six hand grenade-sized eggs a week, and we wondered how her constitution could muster itself to pass these enormous things.

The answer was that she had been designed to do this. Being a hybrid farm bird she was bred not to become broody (it's not productive), to be docile and easy to handle, to produce plenty of meat, and to lay a great many eggs in a short space of time.

A CLOSE CALL

The average working life of a factory-farm chicken is 60 to 70 days, but after a year Mrs. B seemed fit and happy. Then one morning she didn't come barrelling out of the hen-house. As everyone else hunted for breakfast she remained inside. She looked rotten and was slow, mopey, and disinterested in food.

Given her garbage can-style capacity to put away edible things, this was the most worrying sign.

The vet was not encouraging. "She's running a temperature and she's got egg peritonitis," she said.

I had no idea what that was.

"Has she laid any soft eggs recently?" asked the vet.

I said she'd produced a few.

"I think one has broken inside her and is poisoning her system," said the vet.

Lack of calcium is often the cause of soft eggs and we'd studiously mixed special oyster-shell grit in with the chicken feed, which the hens studiously spat out again. This, coupled with a developing physical weakness internally, were the causes of Mrs. Brown's problem. The vet gave her a tumbler-sized injection of antibiotics and equipped me with the inevitable bottle of similar medicine to administer to her when I got home.

Mrs. Brown was very still and quiet.

"She's not at all well, is she?" said the vet. "If I'm honest I don't think she's going to last more than 12 hours. The kindest thing you can do is find her somewhere warm and quiet and keep an eye on her."

I went home thinking that this animal deserved better, brought the cat box containing her into the kitchen, laid some newspaper on the floor and put the box on this. I opened the cat box and put an old margarine carton of water and a few raisins

within easy pecking range, found my laptop, and tried to do some work.

It wasn't easy. I kept looking at the box and speaking to its occupant. Every so often I'd get on my hands and knees, peer inside the box, and gently massage Mrs. Brown's shoulders. She didn't seem to mind this and after a bit stood up, so I left her alone and went back to my work.

About an hour later I heard a "tap-tap-tap" noise, looked up and saw Mrs. B standing on the newspaper and attacking the raisins. I scooped up another handful and she soon got stuck into those as well.

Jane was still at work, so when Mrs. Brown started investigating the usually forbidden kitchen I didn't immediately put a stop to it until, fearing imminent turd terror, I again incarcerated her in the cat box.

Through the mesh door I was viewed with frank resentment, and once Mrs. Brown started to vocalize her displeasure I took the cat box into the garden and released this suddenly reinvigorated animal. She crapped lustily and headed for a flower-bed. That night, rather than watching her die, I put Mrs. Brown back with the others. The following morning she was eager to get out and eat, reluctant to take her medicine and apparently perfectly healthy.

A relapse three weeks later necessitated a return trip to the vet, bringing the total medical expenditure on this $5 chicken

to an insane $75. Later I drove 60 miles from a job to administer some medicine to her, but three years later the chicken with 12 hours to live is still with us, eating hugely, but only very occasionally producing an egg. When she does lay an egg it usually causes some stress on our part as it really isn't good for her.

HEN HAPPINESS

Perhaps this is a waste of money and emotional energy, the indulgence of a deliberately childless, comfortably off couple, but this galumphing, primitive animal with 8,000 feathers has easily given us more entertainment value than we'd have got from spending $75 over 36 months on cigarettes, lifestyle magazines, or some rubbish TV programs that $75-worth of television license would have bought us. We could have gone to a theme-pub restaurant with friends and spent as much on the sort of food people who think food should be faked eat, and then ended up friendless.

Mrs. Brown has seen rather more than her allotted 70 days on the planet (and not spent her time in a shared metal prison), had the chicken equivalent of the sort of medical care lavished on elderly royals, a varied, often exotic diet, subordinates to cower in her presence, and a much younger boyfriend.

She's enjoyed life and we've enjoyed her enjoying it. What more could any of us want?

FURTHER READING

Damerow, Gail, *Storey's Guide to Raising Chickens.* Pownal, Vermont: Storey Press, 1995.

Daniel, Charles and Page Smith, *The Chicken Book.* Athens, Georgia: The University of Georgia Press, reprint 2000.

Lamon, Harry and Rob Slocum, *The Mating and Breeding of Poultry.* Guilford, Connecticut: The Lyons Press, reprint 2003.

Lee, Andy and Pat Foreman, *Chicken Tractor: The Permaculture Guide to Happy Hens and Healthy Soil.* Columbus, Pennsylvania: Good Earth Publications, 1998.

Luttman, Rick and Gail, *Chickens in Your Backyard: A Beginner's Guide.* Emmaus, Pennsylvania: Rodale Press, 1976.

Rossier, Jay. *Living with Chickens.* Guilford, Connecticut: The Lyons Press, 2002.

ORGANIZATIONS

American Poultry Association
133 Millville Street
Mendon, MA 01756
(508) 473-8769
www.ampltya.com

The American Livestock Breeds Conservancy
Box 477
Pittsboro, NC 27313
www.albc-usa.org

American Pasture Poultry Producers Association
5207 70th Street
Chippewa Falls, WI 54729
www.apppa.org

ATTRA Appropriate Technology
Transfer For Rural Areas
PO Box 3657
Fayetteville, Arkansas 72702
www.attra.org

HATCHERIES

ALABAMA
Dixie Poultry Farm
PO Box 506
Saraland, AL 36571
866-868-6069
www.dixiepoultryfarm.com

CALIFORNIA
Belt Hatchery
7272 S. West Ave.
Fresno, CA 93706
559-264-2090
www.belthatchery.com

CONNECTICUT
Hall Brothers Hatchery
PO Box 1026
Norwich, CT 06360
860-886-2421

GEORGIA
K & L Poultry Farm
772 Morris Road
Aragon, GA 30104
706-291-1977
www.klpoultryfarm.com

IDAHO
Dunlap Hatchery
Box 507
Caldwell, ID 83606-0507
208-459-9088

IOWA
Decorah Hatchery
406 W. Water Street
Decorah, IA 52101
563-382-4103
www.decorahhatchery.com

Hoover's Hatchery
PO Box 200
Rudd, IA 50471
800-247-7014
www.hoovershatchery.com

Murray McMurray Hatchery
Box 458, 191 Closz Drive
Webster City, IA 50595-0458
800-456-3280
www.mcmurrayhatchery.com

Sandhill Preservation Center—Heirloom Seeds and Breeds
1878 230th Street
Calamus, IA 52729
563-246-2299

MICHIGAN
Townline Hatchery
PO Box 108
Zeeland, MI 49464
616-772-6514
www.townlinehatchery.com

MINNESOTA
Stromberg's
Box 400
Pine River, MN 56474-0400
800-720-1134
www.strombergschickens.com

MISSISSIPPI
Yoder's Hatchery
256 Jarrell Rd.
Kokoma, MS 39643
601-736-7800

MISSOURI
C. M. Estes Hatchery, Inc.
PO Box 5776
Springfield, MO 65802
417-862-3593
www.esteshatchery.com

Cackle Hatchery
PO Box 529
Lebanon, MO 65536
417-532-4581
www.cacklehatchery.com

Heartland Hatchery
Rt. 1 Box 177-A
Amsterdam, MO 64723
660-267-3679
www.heartlandhatchery.com

Marti Poultry Farm
PO Box 27
Windsor, MO 65360-0027
660-647-3156

McKinney & Govero Poultry
4717 Highway B
Park Hills, MO 63601
573-518-0535 or 573-431-4841
www.mckinneypoultry.com

NEBRASKA
Larry's Poultry Equipment &
Hatchery
PO Box 629
Scottsbluff, NE 69363
800-676-1096
www.larryspoultry.com

NEW MEXICO
Privett Hatchery
PO Box 176
Portales, NM 88130
800-545-3368
www.yucca.net/privetthatchery

NORTH CAROLINA
Seven Oaks Game Farm
7823 Masonboro Sound Road
Wilmington, NC 28409
910-791-5352
www.poultrystuff.com

OHIO
Allen's Poultry &
Gamebird Farm
2165 Alex White Road
Jackson, OH 45640
740-820-4507

Eagle Nest Poultry
Box 504
Oceola, OH 44860
419-562-1993

Mt. Healthy Hatcheries
9839 Winton Road
Mt. Healthy, OH 45231
800-451-5603
www.mthealthy.com

OREGON
Shank's Hatchery
17874 Shank Rd NE
Hubbard, OR 97032-9733
800-344-2449

PENNSYLVANIA
The Easy Chicken Poultry
and Supply
Scott and Kelly Shilala
R.D. 4 Box 464
DuBois, PA 15801
814-583-5374
shilala.homestead.com

Hoffman Hatchery, Inc.
P. O. Box 129
Gratz, PA 17030
717-365-3694
www.hoffmanhatchery.com

Moyer's Chicks, Inc.
266 East Paletown Rd.
Quakertown, PA 18951
215-536-3155
www.moyerschicks.com

Reich Poultry Farms, Inc.
1625 River Road
Marietta, PA 17547
717-426-3411

SOUTH DAKOTA
Inman Hatcheries
PO Box 616
Aberdeen, SD 57402-0616
800-843-1962
www.inmanhatcheries.com

TEXAS
**Ideal Poultry Breeding
Farms, Inc.**
PO Box 591P
Cameron, TX 76520-0591
254-697-6677
www.ideal-poultry.com

WASHINGTON
Harder's Hatchery
624 N. Cow Creek Rd.
Ritzville, WA 99169
509-659-1423

Phinney Hatchery, Inc.
1331 Dell Avenue
Walla Walla, WA 99362-1023
509-525-2602

WISCONSIN
Sunnyside Inc. of Beaver Dam
Hatchery Division
PO Box 452
Beaver Dam, WI 53916
920-887-2122

Utgaard's Hatchery
Box 32
Star Prairie, WI 54026
715-248-3200